WE SHALL NOT BE MOVED

The Women's Factory Strike of 1909

WE SHALL NOT BE MOVED

The Women's Factory Strike of 1909

JOAN DASH

SCHOLASTIC
HARDCOVER

Scholastic Inc. New York

Library of Congress Cataloging-in-Publication Data

Dash, Joan.
We shall not be moved : the women's factory strike of 1909 / Joan Dash.
p.   cm.
Includes bibliographical references and index.
Summary: Describes the conditions that gave rise to efforts to secure
better working conditions for women in the garment industry in
early twentieth-century New York and led to the formation of
the Women's Trade Union League and the first women's strike in 1909.
ISBN 0-590-48409-5 (hardcover)
1. Strikes and lockouts — Clothing trade — New York (N.Y.) — History —
20th century — Juvenile literature.   2. Women clothing workers —
New York (N.Y.) — History — 20th century — Juvenile literature.
[1. Women — Employment — History.   2. Trade unions — Clothing
workers — History.   3. Strikes and lockouts.]
I. Title.
HD5325.C62   1909.N48   1996
331.4'792887'09747109041 — dc20
95-19404   CIP   AC

12 11 10 9 8 7 6 5 4 3 2 1   6 7 8 9/9 0 1/0

Designed by Elizabeth B. Parisi   37
Printed in the U.S.A.
First printing, March 1995

To Shirley Dash,
my steadfast and loving friend

CONTENTS

WE SHALL NOT BE MOVED

The Women's Factory Strike of 1909

1

ON THE EIGHTH FLOOR

They were climbing the narrow staircase, flowing upward by the hundreds — girls, women, a sprinkling of men and boys, but mostly teenaged girls. In their tailored white shirtwaists and long dark skirts, with hair braided or knotted under big picture hats, they looked like students rushing to class, but it was work they were rushing to. Machines awaited them, along with the time clock and the bosses. They had to do their talking now, because once they were inside all talk was forbidden — they could be fined for talking, joking, laughing, or singing. They would talk all the same, of course they would, but softly and warily, their heads turned to one side. What girl of sixteen or eighteen can do a full day's work without once opening her mouth?

When they reached the eighth floor they moved in single file to the time clock. They punched themselves in, glad to have made it in

1

time; being five minutes late meant the loss of half a day's pay.

Taking their hats off, they brought them to the lockers, then headed for their sewing machines, to sit in chairs they rented, just as they paid rent for the lockers that held their hats. They paid for the use of their machines, for their needles, for the thread that went through those needles. In some factories, employees were made to buy their own machine oil, to go out and purchase it although the stores that carried it were hard to find.

Now two hundred and forty workers sat at tables placed in sixteen parallel rows, each row seventy-five feet long, holding fifteen machines. The room itself was high-ceilinged, well-lit, and said to be modern. Fireproof. Run entirely by electricity. The days of the sweatshop were over and this was an up-to-date factory, less than ten years old.

Since most of the workers were recent arrivals from the Jewish townlets, or *shtetls*, of Russia or Poland, it was a marvelous thing to sit at an electrified sewing machine. First a bell rang out, signaling the start of the working day, then there came the humming of the current. A touch of the foot to the treadle, and the needles flashed. The girls bent to their work, feeding fabric to the vibrating needles. The whole floor seemed to vi-

brate beneath them. Although they were made to
pay for this electricity that ran their machines,
they still found it wonderful. In the world they
had left behind there was no such luxury as electricity that sprang to life at the touch of a foot.

The year was 1909. The factory described here
was the Triangle Shirtwaist Company, one of the
largest of some six hundred firms on the Lower
East Side of Manhattan that manufactured shirtwaists. Except for its size, the Triangle was hardly
different from any other. Its methods were typi-
cal, so were its workers, and the way those workers were treated, and the same was true for the
garments they made. Although they varied in
price according to fabric and the quality of deco-
ration, and the styles changed with changes in
fashion, all were instantly recognizable as shirtwaists. Made of white cotton, crisp and clean,
with a high-necked collar, great billowing sleeves,
rows of tucks or pleats down the front, ending in
a fitted waist, they were worn by typists and college students and society matrons as well as shirtwaist workers. The industry that made them
brought in some $50,000,000 a year.

It took ten workers to produce a single shirtwaist. Some sewed sleeves, others stitched cuffs
or collars, made buttonholes, or inserted yokes;
still others worked as trimmers, meaning they

snipped off the ends of threads, hour after hour, day after day, six days a week. Trimmers belonged to the category known as "learners." Girls could be classified as learners even after three years of learning, although there was nothing left to learn. They were paid at most six dollars a week, and made up about a quarter of the workforce.

There was a rush season and a "slack" season; this was the nature of the shirtwaist trade. During rush season workers put in eighty-hour weeks, but at the same rate of pay. A bakery in the garment district made little apple turnovers, and these were what the workers got instead of overtime pay. At other times business was slow and there was no work at all, meaning no pay, but everyone still had to report each morning to the eighth floor of the factory.

In the course of the day one worker or another would have to leave her machine to go to the restroom; the supervisor would follow, rapping on the door to make her hurry. If she took too long she'd be fined, so she did hurry — out of the dark and tiny restroom, whose single toilet stank and sometimes overflowed, and back to the machine. A factory worker named Pauline Newman recalled the time when noiseless rubber heels appeared. "Our employers were the first to use them; you never knew when they would sneak up on you, spying to be sure you did not talk to each other during work hours."

While most workers in the shirtwaist trade were Jews, some were Italians and others, although not many, were "Americans," born in this country. The Jewish workers spoke Yiddish, the Italians spoke Italian, and the Americans spoke a pure, unaccented English, the envy of all the immigrant girls, whose hearts' desire was to speak and dress and act like real Americans.

Bosses and owners often placed Jewish workers next to Italians solely because they had no language in common; then the bosses started stories about race prejudice, hoping to drive them even further apart. There had been strikes. They sputtered up like little flames during the busy season, and were sometimes successful, although they never succeeded in building serious loyalty to the union. But why take chances? If the workers quarreled among themselves it would be harder for the union to organize them.

The workers rarely fought, however. There were squabbles from time to time, this was inevitable. When they were paid on a piecework basis, it sometimes happened that one would complain because another had been given a bigger bundle. Accusations would fly back and forth, claims of unfairness, favoritism. But on the whole they got along well together. There was a spirit of camaraderie, a sense of everyone's being in the same boat. When someone became engaged, for example, the news would find a way of leaping over the language barrier. Ida Shapiro, a shirtwaist maker in one of the smaller factories, remembered, "They gave me a surprise party in the shop. . . . The machines even were decorated. The girls gave me a crystal candlestick and flowers. I had a big wedding and everyone in the shop came. The Italian girls came too." Shop was the usual word for factory.

Because the work was dull and repetitious, workers sang or hummed to themselves to make the day go faster. Some escaped into daydreams. Love, marriage, freedom were what they dreamed about, the world outside the factory, where their lives would belong to themselves, not to the bosses. As Pauline Newman put it, "There was nothing to look forward to, nothing to expect the next day would be better. Someone once asked me, 'How did you survive?' And I told him, what alternative did we have? You stayed and you survived, that's all."

As for the factory owners, except in the smallest shops, they were invisible to the workers, who thought of them as living in another world where they had big houses and fur coats with dollar bills stuffed into the pockets. Accidents, even those that caused serious injury, were not the responsibility of the owners, any more than the workers were their responsibility. They were hands, pairs of hands, paid to operate machines, preferably in total silence.

While the women and girls bent over machines on the eighth floor, work of another sort was going on one floor below — men's work, the kind that paid well. The men were middle-aged and serious-looking, they wore shiny black vests over their white shirts, and some had on *yarmulkes* or skullcaps and some wore black bowler hats that stayed on all day; observant Jewish males kept their heads covered out of respect for the Almighty, who was everywhere.

Here on broad tables, the men known as cutters piled up several dozen layers of fabric, then laid on top of them the pattern for a sleeve or a collar. With a short knife, similar to the kind used by fishermen to gut fish, they sliced out layers of sleeves or collars. Bundles of cut pieces were then sent to the floor above. Only men could be cutters, or bosses, or owners of factories. A determined woman might slowly work her way up, becoming in time a sample maker, even in rare cases a designer. Yet throughout the clothing trades women earned about half what men earned for the same work. And beyond the clothing trades, in the world at large, men were clearly the rulers. They had the vote, therefore they made the laws. Priests, ministers, and rabbis were men, certainly the Almighty was, and Jewish men in their daily prayers thanked Him for not having made them women.

Cutters were the aristocrats of the shirtwaist business, highly skilled workers whose knives could waste money or save it. Bosses and owners respected them. Women workers were another story entirely, partly because they were young; as soon as a girl married she left the factory, returning only if disaster struck.

But the greatest disadvantage of the girls was their being mostly unskilled, easy to replace, above all easily scared. Many were paralyzed by their ignorance of the new country. "I want no experienced girl," one factory owner explained, but only these new immigrants — greenhorns, he called them, who could not speak English — "and they just come from the old country, and I let them work hard, like the devil, for less wages."

They were paid either by the week or by the piece; week-work or piecework, it was all according to which boss had hired them, for hiring was not done by the owner, but by the boss. The subcontractor, he was called, a man who bought or rented a certain number of machines, then hired hands to run them. The owner paid the boss, the boss paid each worker. So two people profited from her labor. Two people tried to drive down her paycheck.

When the lunch bell rang, it brought a precious spell of freedom. Thirty minutes were theirs to do with as they liked, not only to eat what they had brought from home but to move throughout the workroom, talking, singing, even dancing. Talking was the most important part — a way of broadening horizons and exchanging ideas. Newcomers learned from older workers. They practiced their English, they discussed movies, plays, popular songs, hairdos, fashions, and the newness of everything American.

A shirtwaist maker named Fannie Edelman remembered learning the facts of life in the workplace at age sixteen: "Here I became acquainted with a girl who was a little older than I. She told me she was going out with boys and having a good time." Since her mother had explained that even sitting near a man could make her pregnant, Fannie Edelman was shocked to hear that dating was respectable in America. "The girl opened my eyes," she said. "From that time on I began to look at life differently — I started to make the acquaintance of young men."

Work was rarely discussed during lunchtime, since people needed to escape however briefly from work and machines. But their talk often touched on politics, socialism, and economics, meaning the high cost of everything. On six or eight dollars a week, simply staying alive was expensive. The fear of losing their jobs was always with them, as was the fear of lengthy illness. Daily newspapers were full of reports of recent immigrants, men and women alike, who'd been sick, or out of work, or simply unable to adjust to America, and finally "took the gas" — committed suicide by asphyxiation. This, too, would have been on their minds.

An article in *McClure's Magazine*, with the title, "Working-Girls' Budgets," told how girls in the shirtwaist trade managed the business of staying alive. One girl is given the fictional name of Rea Lupatkin. She is nineteen, and like thousands of other young, single Jewish women she has come to America entirely on her own. Working in a shirtwaist factory, Rea earns four dollars for a fifty-six-hour week. Out of this she pays four dollars a month for lodging in a tenement apartment shared with a married couple and their child. She walks forty-five minutes to work each day to save the expense of carfare. Her food costs $2.25 a week. So her regular weekly cost of living is $3.25, leaving seventy-five cents for every other expense. All the same Rea sends an occasional two dollars abroad to her family in Europe.

Another worker, given the name of Betty Lukin, is twenty years old, and has earned from six to ten dollars a week for the past year. Of this she spends three dollars for suppers and a place in a tenement to sleep, and about fifty cents for breakfast and lunch — a roll, and a bit of fruit or candy from a pushcart. Her father is also in New York, but does little to support himself, and there have been many weeks when Betty has deprived herself in order to give him three or four dollars.

In addition to these expenses, she puts aside fifty cents a week for the theater — the Yiddish theater, one of the cultural jewels of the Lower East Side — and ten cents for club dues. As the article points out, "Nearly all the Russian shirtwaist-makers visit the theater and attend clubs and night classes, whatever their wage or their hours of labor. Most of them contribute to the support of a family," whether settled in America, or still in Europe.

Undernourished, living in crowded quarters without proper sanitation, they were at risk for tuberculosis, the most feared of all illnesses on New York's Lower East Side. It struck when times were hard, when the body was already

weakened by malnutrition. People called it the
Jewish disease, the tailors' disease, or the white
plague, and there was no cure other than rest and
good food. Health insurance and welfare were
unknown; a worker stricken with tuberculosis
could hope to enter one of the hospitals main-
tained by Jewish charities, but who would take
care of her family? Again, charity was the only
answer. No one thought of turning to the union
for help.

Yet there was a shirtwaist-makers' union,
Local 25 of the ILGWU — the International
Ladies' Garment Workers' Union, which had
been founded in 1906. Because it was young,
struggling, and incompetently run, Local 25 lived
from hand to mouth, unable at times even to pay
the rent. They dodged the landlord for months;
he finally threw them out. A new hall was found,
there were new financial problems, until one day
they ran out of solutions and agreed to disband.
Covering their charter with a black cloth, they
sneaked quietly out of the building, but once outside it occurred to them that they could continue
to meet, rent-free, if they did so outdoors, so they
reorganized and started over. There were six
members at the time.

By 1909, Local 25 had achieved a membership
of about a hundred, most of them unenthusiastic.

Their bank account consisted of four dollars. Few shirtwaist makers had any faith in this pitiful union, or for that matter very much interest in it. Clara Lemlich, a worker at the Leiserson factory and a member of Local 25's executive board, was an exception. People said she was "on fire for the union."

During the summer of 1909, two hundred employees had walked out of a firm called Rosen Brothers. Five weeks later the owners reached an agreement with the union, but by then the strike had spread to several other factories, including Leiserson's. Clara Lemlich was pulled from the picket line, jumped on by hired thugs, thoroughly beaten up, and sent to the hospital with three broken ribs. The Yiddish-language newspapers gave daily accounts of the state of her health.

Clara Lemlich was an experienced worker, well-paid, earning three times as much as most women in the shirtwaist trade. She was striking for the others, she said, and not only for better hours and wages, but for human dignity. For an end to the series of petty humiliations that were part of a shirtwaist maker's daily life.

One example was the bundle system. The boss gave a bundle of sleeves, collars, or buttonholes to a worker, and when she returned the finished bundle, he handed her a ticket to be converted to cash on payday. The ticket was a tiny scrap of paper, easily lost, and without it the girl had no claim whatever on her pay. Even when she held on to her ticket there were frequent "mistakes" in pay envelopes, and the process of getting them fixed was so complex that hardly anyone tried.

Clocks were speeded up at lunchtime to shorten the thirty minutes of freedom. Toward the end of the day some bosses covered the clock, especially during the busy season, and the workers were compelled to eat their apple turnovers with one hand while running the machine with the other.

In the smaller shops, located in little lofts, floors sometimes collapsed from the weight of too many machines and people. Shop fires were common. So was sexual aggression by bosses and foremen. Accounts given by workers about factory life are full of stories of men who pinched, patted, groped, or even grabbed a girl and pulled her into an office. One worker remembered how she'd been afraid of her boss: "He tried to hug me and I was so ashamed because I didn't know what to say or do. No man had ever kissed me except my father before." A worker who rebuffed a boss could be fired, in fact anyone could be fired, with or without a cause.

These were some of the indignities Clara Lemlich had in mind when she led her fellow workers out on strike — lies, insults, petty humiliations, all of which had to be swallowed down, gulped like the apple turnovers, while one hand ran the machine.

The day finally came to an end. The foreman rang the quitting bell, machinists pulled the switches. Workers jumped to their feet, yawned, stretched, and started talking again, filling the factory with human sounds. After finding their hats, they filed out one by one through the door that led to the staircase, where a watchman waited while they emptied their purses. The owners suspected everyone of thievery; even long hair might conceal stolen sleeves or collars. There was a fashion for "rats," big puffy pompadours, and the watchman had been instructed to be on the lookout for oversize hairdos.

Then they went downstairs and started home, some walking, some treating themselves to the trolley. Those who passed one or another of the factories on strike would have seen the picket lines, where strikers handed out leaflets to workers as they came through factory doors. But what use was a union that couldn't protect Clara Lemlich, one of its own leaders? Of course it was wonderful to fight so resolutely for social justice, but it was also pointless. The owners were big important men, powerful, with powerful friends. What did the union amount to?

During the summer of 1909, then, there was little reason to suspect that within months the shirtwaist workers and their union were going to bring a multimillion-dollar industry to its knees. Most of the credit would belong to the workers themselves, the rest to those who came to their aid, of whom some would be "ladies," meaning women of leisure. One would be Mary Dreier, a member of a prominent Brooklyn family. The others would also be women — a battalion of women, young and old, with little in common beyond the fact of their being women.

Many had never before seen the Lower East Side, or met a Yiddish-speaking factory girl face-to-face.

2

THE HOMES OF THE SHIRTWAIST GIRLS

In the early years of the century, immigrants poured into the United States at the rate of over a million a year, mostly from Southern or Eastern Europe. Of these, only a small proportion were Jews, typically 100,000 a year. But they tended to settle in one small neighborhood, the Lower East Side of Manhattan, wave after wave of them living in each other's pockets, until by 1909 it had become the most crowded place in the world. A single block might house as many as 3,700 souls.

Although other immigrants lived there as well — Italians, Syrians, Slovaks, the Germans, Irish, and Poles — it was the Jewish presence that gave the East Side its unmistakable character. Here they clung together, speaking their own language, seeing faces like their own, eating the foods that were familiar to them. On Hester Street, at the neighborhood's heart, they had created a vast open-air marketplace that seemed to have been moved like a stage set from some *shtetl* in Russia or Poland. Pavements were lined on both sides by an unbroken double row of pushcarts, these pushcarts overflowing into lesser markets along the pavements of side streets. Wagons and horse-drawn carts were jostled day and night by bearded old men, and bustling housewives with long dark aprons covering black skirts, some with wigs on, some with kerchiefs tied over their heads. There were countless children in unstoppable motion, toddlers holding tight to their mothers, little girls dancing to hurdy-gurdy music, also beggars, piles of refuse, spoiled food, the droppings of horses. Noise. Loud voices comparing prices or urging people to buy, buy. Not from him but from me.

The owner of a cart filled with grapes and pears would call out in a shriek: Good fruit! Good fruit! Bargains! Another had fish for sale, big and little, light fish and dark fish, bluefish and whitefish. Still another offered huge loaves of bread, black as tar, known as Polish bread. Cucumber pickles floated in salty brine, smoked and pickled meats peppered the air with powerful smells, herrings by the barrelful waited to be chopped up and eaten with onions. There was both new and used clothing, corsets, shoes, skullcaps, men's suits, as well as washboards, cook-pots, Sabbath candles, and whatever else was needed for the Jewish body and spirit. The market went on well into the night, when it was lit by hundreds of flaming torches.

In Europe the pushcarts would have been planted in mud. Here they had the cobblestoned street underfoot, and the free skies of America overhead. People could move uptown to the Bronx whenever they wanted or could afford it; they could leave for Chicago, even California. In America, no laws dictated where a Jew had the right to live.

But even in free America there were those who took offense at the very existence of the Jewish East Side, a place they believed to be darkly menacing. According to the *New York Times*, "This neighborhood . . . is the eyesore of New York and perhaps the filthiest place on the western continent. It is impossible for a Christian to live there because he will be driven out, either by blows, or the dirt and stench. Cleanliness is an unknown quantity to these people. They cannot be lifted to a higher plane because they do not want to be."

There was worse to come. In 1908, Theodore Bingham, the police commissioner of New York City, wrote an article entitled, "Foreign Criminals in New York." He claimed that half the criminals in the city were Jews, "burglars, firebugs, pickpockets and highway robbers."

In response to this outburst, mass meetings of protest flared up in the Lower East Side halls. The Yiddish press exploded; every Jewish organization denounced Bingham as an anti-Semite. Leaders of the long-established Jewish community — such as Louis Marshall, the great constitutional lawyer and Jacob Schiff, the financier — protested more sedately, and within weeks Bingham apologized, "frankly and without reservation."

Although the uproar subsided it was never forgotten. Within the crowded dwellings of the immigrant community people asked themselves if they could ever shake off the squalor and filth of their surroundings — if they would ever be truly welcome in America.

Behind the Hester Street market, and in the streets on all sides of it for blocks and blocks, the wooden tenement buildings loomed. Seven or eight stories high, there were many with toilets only in the courtyard below. Even the best and newest tenements had no more than two toilets to a floor, where a nail hammered into the wall held cut-up newspaper, and no light came in except from the candle brought by the occupant. Rooms were dark, airless, often windowless, noisy with the movements of rats and cockroaches. In summer, hoping to catch a breath of air, people slept on the roof or the front steps or the flimsy fire escapes, which were usually clogged with broken furniture.

Every single one of these tenement buildings was a firetrap. A housing reformer, Lawrence Veiller, referred to the district as "The City of Living Death," where "the working-man is housed worse than in any other city in the civilized world."

There was no such luxury as a room of one's own, for apartments had to be shared with paying boarders. Sometimes the beds themselves had to be shared. There were rooms, including kitchens, whose floors were covered wall to wall with mattresses, each serving two or three, male boarders in one room, women in another, and it was not unheard of for people to sleep in shifts, those who worked at night taking turns with those who worked by day. When a household ran out of mattresses, two kitchen chairs with a board laid across them served as a bed.

Water came either from a spigot outdoors in the courtyard, or a kitchen faucet — cold water, that had to be heated for the weekly bath, which was taken in a portable tub placed in the kitchen near the stove. Clothes were boiled on the stove, washed with homemade soap, hung out to dry on lines that ran back and forth across air-shafts, then boiled again with starch, dried again, and finally dampened and ironed. The laundry of boarders went through the same process. Who washed this mountain of laundry? Usually the mother, with the help of the eldest daughter after a day's work in the factory, but some female boarders washed their own, also after a full day's work.

Many of these Jewish immigrants had come to America with little education, since in Eastern Europe the universities were essentially closed to them, and in some areas the schools were closed as well. Jewish communities supported their own schools, with religious studies the chief subject. In the new world they took whatever work they could get. Longing for those they had left behind in Europe, they sent their dollars to Europe. Living in airless tenements, they ate cheap food and wore cheap clothing and shared their miserable homes with strangers. Some gave up and returned to Russia, others committed suicide, or disappeared into one of the tuberculosis hospitals. All the same, to hundreds of thousands of newcomers on the run from anti-Semitism and murderous pogroms, the organized massacres of Jewish populations, this was the "goldene medina," the golden land, and the Lower East Side, with Hester Street at its heart, was their promised city.

About half of those who lived here found work in the garment trade, where Jews from earlier migrations were already in business, some on a large scale, others so small that a Yiddish-language newspaper referred to them as "small 'insects' of manufacturers."

Just as their factory lives were separate from those of the men, so were the home lives of Jewish girls and women. Boys played baseball, to the dismay of fathers who wanted them only to study; they explored the streets in packs, defying Gentile boys from other neighborhoods. The streets were their chance to break away for a few hours from parental expectations, the place where they tested themselves against the challenge of the real America.

Girls played jacks or hopscotch or jump rope, and did no exploring. Under the watchful eyes of Jewish mothers, little girls learned how to be mothers themselves, observing the dietary laws, keeping the holy days, and honoring the Sabbath on Saturday. Although religious practice was far less strict than in Europe, a Jewish family was still a Jewish family, where things were done a certain way.

When a girl reached sixteen she went to work — that was it, no question about it; her wages were needed to support the family. Most boys stayed on to finish high school, however, and some went further. "The city college is practically filled with Jewish pupils," says a book published by the Young People's Missionary Movement, referring to New York's City College — tuition-free and open only to the brightest students when they happened to be boys.

Girls with a hunger for education could put aside a little something from their earnings in the hope of finishing their schooling later on. In the meanwhile, they could go to night school or to the public library. And there were other ways to learn about America, painlessly, almost effortlessly. Department stores were treasure houses of learning; by walking uptown to Macy's or Bloomingdale's, they could ride the moving staircases that took them past floor after floor displaying wonders — clothing, furniture, pianos, books — the stores themselves filled with people who moved freely about. The girls could touch whatever they liked. They could try on clothes, or open a book and leaf through it. They could pretend these wonders were theirs, that they, too, lived like real Americans, owners of books and pianos.

The Lower East Side was densely packed with ice-cream parlors, a strictly American food they had never tasted before, or even seen. Movies were another novelty, still silent, but with a powerful fascination for East Side immigrants. Families went to the movies together to watch American history unfold before their eyes. A girl could learn what Paul Revere did, and who gave the Boston Tea Party, and how thrillingly wild the Wild West was. She could see Americans driving about in automobiles, drinking in taverns, bashing one another in the face with pies. Hundreds of people waited in line before the movie houses, where shows lasted half an hour, and could be watched over and over.

On the pushcarts, or in the shops of the Lower East Side, a factory worker could buy cheap clothing that transformed her overnight into someone hardly distinguishable at a distance from a real American. This was another of the country's miracles. The machinery of mass production made it possible for those who had stepped off the boat in the clothing of peasants — ragged homemade sweaters, their legs in thick woolen stockings, dark shawls sheltering their heads — to dress the way royalty dressed in the old country.

There was no question about their loving

pretty clothes. As Clara Lemlich said, "we're all human, all of us girls, and we're young. We like new hats as well as any other young women. Why shouldn't we?" To buy that new hat, "even if it hasn't cost more than fifty cents, means that we have gone for weeks on two cent lunches — dry cake and nothing else." But they bought the hats, and cherished them. Unlike the black shawls that belonged to the Old World, large and elaborate hats were part of being an "allrightnik," a real American.

While their parents had come to escape anti-Semitism and poverty, the daughters had other reasons as well, based on the belief that to be American meant to be modern. The modern world was mostly a rumor in Eastern Europe, but a tremendously alluring one. It had to do with personal freedom, and growth, and making choices for oneself. In the modern world a girl could marry for love, instead of having to settle for the boy chosen by her parents. Schools were open to American girls, even colleges were. And it was well known that American men treated women respectfully, not like inferiors, but as finer and purer beings.

This was the message of America, if not to the mothers, then to the daughters. Yet even the mothers had had a degree of freedom in the Old

World that set them apart from the Irish, Italian, or Syrian women who were their neighbors now.

In their old-world lives, men were expected to devote themselves to religious study, the best and highest of callings. Few were able to get by without some shopkeeping or peddling, but they tended to spend much of their time in the Beth Hamidrash, the house of study, and leave serious money-getting in the hands of the women. This meant that wives usually ran the small businesses that kept the family going; some became peddlers, or sold homemade goods in the marketplace. They had no voice in community affairs, just as they had none in religious affairs. As the prayer book made clear, they were less worthy than men, yet they worked and they earned; it was expected of them.

When they reached America these traditional attitudes came with them. They managed pushcarts on Hester Street, or sewed at home, making garments or parts of garments to be sold to factories nearby. With the burden of the boarders also on her shoulders, the Jewish mother worked by day and by night. The family and its future were what she worked for; they were woven into her dreams over the sewing machine or the cookstove.

A few of the women, whether mothers or

daughters, had been active politically in the old country, where they belonged to socialist youth groups in the big cities. They retained their faith in the power of socialism to set things right, and this, too, was part of their dreams for America.

Clara Lemlich was both a dreamer and a doer, a slender girl of not quite twenty, with deepset eyes and a great deal of dense black hair, whose brother described her as intensely single-minded: "If she is to make anything she must make it, that is all. She was always that way in Russia and here. If she has to finish a book of three hundred pages or three thousand, she does not anything else until she finishes that — eating, sleeping, nothing matters. And when she works she works, and when she strikes she strikes. That is Clara."

She had been born on the outskirts of a small Ukrainian village where the two-grade schoolhouse did not accept Jews. Her parents were shopkeepers, her father a Jewish scholar as well. What Clara wanted was to learn to read books, real books, the kind read by Russian students, but her parents refused to have her learn Russian. They didn't want to hear it or see it — it was the language of the oppressors. Besides, a girl's education was supposed to consist of enough Hebrew to stumble through the prayers, enough written Yiddish to compose a letter, and a smattering of arithmetic. They told her to forget about Russian.

So Clara went into the little village, made buttonholes in the tailor shops, and handed her earnings over to students who taught her to read Russian. When her father found the books he threw them into the fire, but the damage was already done. By the time the family fled to America in 1903, Clara Lemlich was familiar with revolutionary literature that declared the rights of workers, even women workers.

In New York she became a shirtwaist girl, put in an eleven-hour day, then gulped a glass of milk and ran to the public library, where she studied till closing time; only then did she permit herself to eat the supper her mother had prepared for her. It was Clara's intention to become a doctor, an intention never fulfilled because she was always too busy with conditions in the factory. One day she went with a group of young people to the office of the *Jewish Daily Forward*, to learn how to form a union, and that was how Local 25 of the ILGWU began. With a girl getting fed up. An ordinary working girl, infected by dreams. "I had fire in my mouth," she said later. "What did I know about trade unionism? Audacity — that was all I had — audacity."

Most of the shirtwaist girls were not yet infected. They had reason to believe that the union, their union, Local 25, which was supposed to serve makers of shirtwaists who were mostly female, neither needed nor wanted them. Clara Lemlich was on its executive board, so were some other women, but all the paid officials were men. And the ILGWU — the parent union of ladies' garment workers — was known to be a male stronghold.

Union meetings took place at night, in the smoke-filled cafes that served as the universities of the ghetto. Intellectuals preached brotherhood and Marxism, Judaism, and socialism in the cafes, where the atmosphere was boisterous, and most teenaged girls felt unwelcome. Besides, fathers and boyfriends disapproved of their going out on the streets at night.

As for the Italian girls, they were a minority in the Jewish ghetto of the East Side, suffering from isolation as well as the language barrier. Ruled by fathers and priests who feared the union and the independence it might bring to young women, Italian girls tended to be timid and obedient. They took no interest whatever in Local 25. The native-born girls, the "Americans," considered themselves superior to the squabbles of immigrant foreigners, and they, too, ignored the union.

It must be pointed out that union officials, from the lowest to the highest, including Samuel Gompers, who headed the AFL, the American Federation of Labor, held similar opinions — that women didn't belong in the union, and didn't belong in the factory to begin with. In any case they were there just for a brief interval between school and marriage. Even while they were working they did it only for "pin money." The unions had more serious matters on their minds than organizing female fly-by-nights.

These beliefs were never expressed in public. In public, Gompers and other union leaders claimed they were fighting for the rights of all workers, female as well as male, black as well as white.

3

AN ALLIANCE IS FORMED

The summer and early autumn of 1909, when strikes flared up at Rosen Brothers and Leiserson's, was a season of restlessness. Soon workers were picketing at several of the smaller firms, carrying placards that bore such slogans as, WE ARE STRIKING FOR HUMAN TREATMENT, or, WE STRIKE FOR JUSTICE. By September there was strike talk at Triangle.

Until that point the chief weapon of factory owners had been the use of so-called "special police" to guard their premises. One newspaper referred to them as "gorillas." Most were thugs and some were known criminals, and their true function was to terrify the picket line.

A group of strikers would be walking two by two before the factory door, waiting for workers to leave at quitting time. Because these workers had been hired to replace those on strike, they were called strikebreakers or, less politely, "scabs."

When the strikebreakers came out, the picket line would offer leaflets explaining the reasons for the strike, and imploring them to quit work and join the union.

A reporter for the *New York Sun,* describing the picket line at Leiserson's, tells what happened next: "Of a sudden, around the corner came a dozen tough-looking customers. . . . 'Stand fast, girls,' called Clara (Lemlich), and then the thugs rushed the line, knocking Clara to her knees, striking at the pickets, opening the way for a group of frightened scabs to slip through. . . . There was a confused melee of scratching, screaming girls and fist-swinging men and then a patrol wagon arrived. The thugs ran off as the cops pushed Clara and two other badly beaten girls into the wagon."

At one factory, gorillas beat two of the pickets so badly that an ambulance had to be called. Another day a boy was beaten, and for ten days could not open his mouth even to eat. "One girl's boss came to her home at seven in the morning in the company of a detective," a striker recalled, "entered her bedroom and ordered the detective to arrest her. She began to scream and the neighbors came . . . and insisted that the girl be given time to dress."

Where were the real police when "special police" were attacking strikers? Often they were right there, stationed at factory gates beside the gorillas. Although New York State law upheld the right of peaceful picketing, the police force was thoroughly corrupt and had been for decades. It was said that anyone could get a man on the beat to look the other way by giving him a box of cigars with a $100 bill in it.

Most judges and magistrates were equally corrupt; so was much of New York City government, which for generations had been ruled from Tammany Hall, headquarters of a political organization that specialized in bribery and favoritism. When the Irish policemen took shirtwaist girls before the magistrates, they were usually fined — for speaking to strikebreakers, for loitering, for simply being out in the street. Magistrate Olmstead told a group of bruised and bleeding picketers, "You are on strike against God and nature, whose prime law is that man shall earn his bread by the sweat of his brow."

So the story of that summer was one of strikes in several factories, the strikers harassed by thugs, police and judges alike siding with the owners. Triangle workers attended strike meetings, but even the meetings were not safe from gorillas or spies. One evening, when officials of United Hebrew Trades came to speak to the workers, they did so behind locked doors and with window shades drawn.

In September, Triangle's entire workforce walked out, men and women alike, even some subcontractors, in an extraordinary show of unity. The owners licked their wounds and wondered what to do next.

All this time workers from the struck shops had of course been joining Local 25, which now had hundreds of new members. Although strikes were common enough in the garment trades, they hardly ever took place during the summer, the slack season when jobs were scarce. Local 25 also debated its next move.

Triangle's owners then decided that more extreme measures were called for. They were in a cutthroat business here in America, which was not the Old Country, where a man was judged by his Jewish scholarship. In America success came from piling up money, and to pile up money you had to make shirtwaists faster and cheaper than the factory next door. They believed this could not be done with a union breathing down their necks, telling them what wages to pay, whom they could hire, and how to run their factory.

Triangle's next move was to hire a number of prostitutes, "fancy ladies from the Allen Street red-light district," in the words of the *Sun*, to stand at factory gates beside the gorillas. They were there to taunt and insult the picketers, to show them that by picketing, by risking violence, arrest, and jail, they had so lowered themselves that society classed them with streetwalkers.

If it seems strange today that picketing should turn a young woman into an outcast, it must be remembered that this was an era when one of the arguments used against giving women the vote was that the polling places were unsavory. Men of every description, even so-called bums, gathered there. The delicate flower of womanhood must be protected from all contact with streets and polling places.

"Streetwalker is one of the terms that the police and the thugs apply daily to the strikers," a journalist wrote, "in fact it has become in their vocabulary almost synonymous with striker." The word was doubly hurtful to the shirtwaist makers, not only because of the insult, but because they were slum-dwellers who lived with the daily knowledge of the street and its dangers. Many would have known of a woman driven by hunger to prostitution, so that the possibility was real and frightening to them.

The Triangle owners had to rethink their strategy when six prostitutes attacked two young pickets, threw them to the ground, and beat them

until their faces streamed with blood. Their
shrieks brought workers in the office buildings
and factories of the neighborhood to the windows; soon the whole street was picketing in
protest.

In less than two days the prostitutes were re-
moved, but the thugs remained. The strikers
were afraid of them; they were afraid of the police, of the mysterious courtroom where only
English was spoken. Yet the strikes went on. The
Jewish workers threw themselves into this new
cause with a fervor that was not always reason-
able.

Meanwhile another player had arrived on
the scene of battle, the Women's Trade Union
League. Its most conspicuous members were
"ladies," well-educated, middle-aged, and rich,
and they had come to the Lower East Side several years earlier in order to be of service to factory women.

The League was born of the same reform
movement that gave rise to Hull House, a neighborhood center in the slums along Chicago's Polk
and Halsted streets. Here Jane Addams, who
grew up in a small town in Illinois, had established a settlement that drew together working
people and progressive reformers, and inspired
other settlement houses in other big-city slums.

The reformers were mostly "ladies," as were members of the League, and their mission reflected changes in American society that had been having a dramatic effect on the status of women.

The country used to be mainly agricultural, a landscape mostly of farms and villages. In the second half of the nineteenth century, thanks to a remarkable series of inventions, the national landscape became increasingly industrial. Factories were turning out a seemingly endless supply of low-cost goods that transformed daily life: ready-made clothing, canned food, store-bought bread, luxuries such as furniture of golden oak, and new necessities, refrigerators, steam heat, indoor plumbing. A firm named Sears, Roebuck and Company, calling itself "The Cheapest Supply House on Earth," promised to send products by mail to the remotest sections of the nation.

For women of the new middle class, the families of manufacturers, businessmen, and salaried professionals, these changes were sometimes disastrous. Their grandmothers had baked bread, churned butter, and cooked and sewed for large households, but these occupations had vanished except on the farm, and farming was no longer the usual way of life. With servants to care for the children and manage the household, middle-class women were left with nothing to do now, no known function except as consumers — buying what factories made. So they dressed themselves in multiple layers of clothing, chemises, drawers, corsets, corset-covers, under several petticoats. They overfurnished their homes, created elaborate embroideries, and visited one another. Whole weeks could be used up by a succession of visits to women exactly like themselves. Rheta Dorr, later a member of the Women's Trade Union League, longed to escape from this life of overdressed visiting — "I for one wanted to get out into the world of real things."

Women like Rheta Dorr joined the women's clubs of the 1880s and 1890s. Sometimes they formed study groups, turning their attention to botany, history, art, or literature. Others inspected local factories to see how workers were treated. There was a growing fascination with women who worked, a belief that work itself could be liberating, even factory work.

By the turn of the century one worker in five was female, partly because in many factory jobs a woman's skill was equal to a man's, yet she could be hired for much less. She was also easier to exploit than a man. Somehow the spirit of rebellion seemed to be lacking in women.

Two sisters-in-law, Marie and Bessie Van Vorst,

took jobs in a succession of factories, such as can-
neries and Southern textile mills, and wrote a
book, *The Woman Who Toils: Being the Experience of
Two Ladies as Factory Girls.* In a pickle factory
Marie was taken off the assembly line and told to
scrub floors on her hands and knees, which she
found humiliating. She went to a department
where men were working, and they, too, had
been instructed to clean floors — but they stood,
and they used hoses and long-handled mops. And
when she asked for an explanation, one of the
men told her, "What scrubbing can't be done with
mops ain't going to be done by me." He added
that the women wouldn't have to scrub, either, if
they had the guts to say so.

Marie Van Vorst concluded that the men were
united because all were breadwinners, while the
women worked for varied reasons; some were
breadwinners, others worked only for luxuries,
still others fell somewhere between the two.
There would be no strikes by women, she
claimed, so long as the question of wages was not
equally vital to all.

By the early 1900s, a small nucleus of social reformers came to believe that the one sure way to
improve the lot of factory women was through
the unions. It was a new and bold approach, and
went totally against the grain of middle-class

thinking. People who owned businesses or property were deeply suspicious of unions, which
gave rise to strikes, thus threatening private
property and the "inalienable" right of business
to do what business was supposed to do, make
money.

But this little group of progressives were determined to proceed with their experiment. Would
the AFL — the major body uniting American
local unions — join in and help? Of course they
would, said Samuel Gompers. Would the AFL
hire women organizers? Without question, Gompers replied.

This new organization, the Women's Trade
Union League, came to life in 1903. According to
their constitution, the executive board was to in-
clude equal numbers of working women, and
"allies," meaning middle-class reformers. There
were other organizations devoted to the welfare
of factory women, but it was the League, and
only the League, that aimed to unionize them,
and to do so hand in hand with the workers themselves.

The AFL made a short-lived attempt to hire a
woman organizer, but she left after a few months
and was never replaced. Gompers assured the
League they would be "courteously welcomed" at
national AFL conventions, yet refused to seat

them as delegates. And while the women were permitted to use the phrase "Endorsed by the AFL" on their letterhead, the Federation never gave them more than token financial aid.

Fortunately for the League there were other ways to finance a young, struggling organization. A Brooklyn-born heiress by the name of Margaret Dreier came to the attention of some League leaders. She was in her late thirties, impressively tall, with vast energies and a romantic nature, and she longed to do important work in the world of real things.

Her younger sister, Mary, who adored her, described "the intelligence, enthusiasm, youth and beauty which were united in Margaret's personality," but did not fail to note that her sister was self-centered and domineering. Mary also joined the League, for she, too, longed to give her life to some important cause without knowing how, or where, or what form it would take. Unlike Margaret, Mary was not domineering. Blue-eyed, with wispy hair and the shy, self-effacing manner of one who lacked confidence in herself, she was terrified of public speaking.

The older sister, Margaret, fell in love with Raymond Robins, a social reformer who had made a fortune in mining. A month after they met in 1905 they were engaged; two months after that they married and moved to Chicago, now the League's national headquarters. They found a cold-water flat on the top floor of a tenement building. It was heated only by a coal-burning stove, so they froze in the winter and sweltered all summer, and lived on ten dollars a week because that was how their neighbors lived. Margaret Dreier Robins became the League's national president in 1907, and for the next twenty years devoted both herself and her sizable fortune to it.

Mary Dreier was elected president of the New York chapter, and gave herself to the cause of working women as selflessly as her older sister had. And when she, too, fell in love with Raymond Robins she confessed her love to him, in a series of passionate and painful letters that were kept secret from Margaret.

Raymond Robins, a man of great charm and intelligence, persuaded his sister-in-law to "sacrifice her passion on the altar of reform." The secret correspondence remained secret, along with Mary Dreier's poetry, mediocre poetry, according to one historian, and she never married, but then many of the women reformers were unmarried. Photographs capture the intensity of her expression, her blue eyes wary, her face pale and tight. She was doing what she had promised, sacrificing her passion on the altar of reform.

As head of the New York chapter of the League it was Mary Dreier's task to sell factory women on unionism, while at the same time selling unions on the value of unskilled female members. Neither task was likely to be easy. The unions were indifferent, even hostile, and the workers sensed this hostility. Also, communicating with the factory women proved to be difficult, since they spoke little English and were generally unfamiliar with American industrial society. They had never before met middle-class reformers, and seemed unsure what the "ladies" wanted of them. Yet one way or another their trust would have to be gained. After establishing an unpretentious office in the factory district, the League set out to do so.

At first they gave picnics, teas, and dances — "sociables," they were called. But these gatherings tended to be stiff and awkward, and were also beside the point. Unionism was the point. The League added more aggressive tactics, and finally went out into the streets. Every day at noon, and again in the early evening, League speakers set up platforms, unfurled their banners, and preached the gospel of trade unionism near factory doors.

They were proud of their street rallies, of doing what "ladies" never dared to do. Soon the New York League was helping to organize workers in a number of trades — dressmaking, hat-trimming, and buttonhole-making. The local unions they formed rarely lasted more than a season or two, partly because the League knew nothing whatever about organizing; they had to teach themselves, relying on AFL guidelines.

There were other matters they knew nothing about. They were unaware that their headquarters had an atmosphere of gentility that could be stifling to working people. Afternoon tea had become an honored custom. Large portions of culture were made available, classes in folk dance, gymnastics, and debating, offered to anyone with a union card. Dance recitals were held, and choral groups formed. In addition, allies took a personal interest in their working-class members, often financing vacations and medical treatment, even helping them to complete their educations. And all this warm-hearted generosity was painful to the workers.

Pauline Newman, first a factory worker, then a League organizer, wrote to her friend Rose

Schneiderman, "My work is horrible! The keeping sweet all the time and pleading for aid from the 'dear ladies' and the ministers is simply sickening."

Another worker-member, Leonora O'Reilly, left the League twice and then rejoined it, for the same reasons. "Contact with the lady does harm in the long run," she once said. "It gives the wrong standard." It was as if the workers had no culture of their own and must be spoon-fed the culture of others. Throughout the League's existence there would be dissension between the two halves, yet they held together, united by a common purpose and by ties of genuine affection. Mary Dreier, in particular, was loved by all for her honesty and simplicity.

In the summer and early autumn of 1909, ladies of the League marched on picket lines in front of Leiserson's and Triangle, as tireless as shirtwaist makers half their age. The strike was still on at both places, and as September gave way to October the violence intensified, especially at Triangle. Joe Zeinfeld, the chairman of their strike committee, was attacked by thugs in front of the factory, punched and kicked until he fell to the pavement unconscious, his face cut up so badly that it required thirty stitches. Three men arrested one morning for shooting up a saloon turned out to be employed as strikebreakers by Triangle.

Triangle sued the Yiddish-language *Jewish Daily Forward* because of "the assistance that paper renders the striking waist makers during the present battle." However the rest of New York knew little about the battle, the thugs, or the beatings. The rest of New York knew little about shirtwaists for that matter, except as an article of clothing.

During this same period, officials of Local 25 began to realize that the shop-by-shop strikes weren't going to work. To get what they wanted — humane treatment, and justice, and better wages — they would have to tie up the entire trade during the busy season. This meant simultaneous walkouts throughout the shirtwaist business.

The idea gathered momentum. Officers of Local 25 started using the phrase "general strike," although it was not entirely accurate. A general strike usually means one involving all workers in a broad geographical area, or else in a large industrial area — all farm workers in the state of California, for example. But this was how they spoke about it among themselves. A general strike, affecting every factory that made shirtwaists.

Since there were about six hundred such factories, employing well over thirty thousand workers, and only a small percentage belonged to the union, it was a wild idea. There had never been such a strike anywhere in the garment district. Furthermore the ILGWU itself was only nine years old. Five years earlier it had had a respectable membership; one year later it was on the brink of dissolution. Now the ILGWU was fighting its way back. But a general strike?

Their leaders disapproved of strikes to begin with, and a general strike at this point in their history would be folly. A general strike required the broad-based membership they would have in time, but for now the young people of Local 25 had better calm down.

There was a meeting of Local 25's executive board, Clara Lemlich among them. They voted approval of this general strike. It was still seen as a gamble, a shot in the dark. But if — if — they managed somehow to pull it off they would need both money and publicity. The League was plentifully supplied with well-connected women, capable of calling public attention to the struggle, and many were very rich. They expressed their willingness to join hands with the young people of Local 25 in the possible general strike.

The ILGWU was not impressed. One observer

noted that John Dyche, the ILGWU's national secretary, "was very snooty about this alliance between high-brow 'butters in' and 'irresponsible little girls.'"

Meanwhile there were many factories where strike talk was never heard, and many workers totally indifferent to the possibility of a strike, general or otherwise. As far as they were concerned, nothing was going to change because a handful of workers saw fit to march up and down before some factory doors, and for weeks nothing did change.

Then, on the morning of November 4, with Mary Dreier doing picket duty in front of the Triangle, she happened to speak to a young woman worker going in through the factory gate, telling her there was a strike against Triangle, and begging her not to be a strikebreaker.

The woman grew angry. She hit Miss Dreier, then turned to the policeman who stood nearby and told him to arrest this person for harassing her, which he did. When they reached the Mercer Street station house, the woman told the officer behind the desk that Miss Dreier had said, "I will split your head open if you try to go to work."

The officer took one look at mild-faced Mary Dreier and knew she had never threatened to split open anyone's head. Besides, she had already identified herself as president of the New York chapter of the League, and given her home address in a fashionable part of Brooklyn. She was released without further questions, as the arresting officer was heard to mutter, "Why didn't you tell me you was a lady? I'd never have arrested you for the world."

The next day two policemen were put on duty in front of the Triangle, to see that the handful of young strikers did no harm to the factory or its workers. But city newspapers had caught wind of this event, the arrest of a lady, followed by the apology of the officer once he heard who she was. Working women could be hauled in for picketing, it seemed, but not society women. *The New York Times* made it a front-page story.

Reporters followed it up for the next ten days, pouring out the details of starvation wages, the bullying, the fines, the payments for needles and thread, for chairs, electricity, and machine oil. Now everyone knew. The public at large read accounts of factory life with their morning news, along with Miss Dreier's statement that her arrest "was only the latest in a series of outrages, in which police have always taken the side of employers . . . even when the pickets have been beaten in the presence of police."

Many more workers joined the union — they,

too, read newspapers — until there were several thousand enlisted in Local 25. The remote possibility of a general strike seemed slightly less remote now. If it succeeded, the ILGWU would gain enormously. It would have the beginnings of an important mass organization, while what it had now was mainly potential.

But John Dyche remained skeptical; he suggested forming a committee to investigate conditions in the factories. Others pointed out that general strikes in unorganized trades invariably failed, and here the workers were women — known to be impulsive by nature, undisciplined, impossible to organize. Not only women, but young. Hardly more than children. Winter was just around the corner; at the first snowflake these children would surely run for cover.

All the same, Local 25 was determined to gather as many workers as possible and sound them out. Local 25 consulted its partner, the League. Would they share the cost of renting a hall? The League agreed.

In the history of American labor, no band of women had ever borne the brunt of a large-scale strike, but it seemed the time had come to try.

4

"IF I TURN TRAITOR"

A crowd of three thousand pushed their way into an East Side assembly hall; hundreds more were sent to overflow halls nearby. Leaflets distributed by the union had urged them to come to this meeting in order to find out "when the general strike will be called," but one of the workers remembered wondering whether anything at all would happen that night.

Although most had never before attended a union meeting, they had seen union circulars, which tended to be written on a note of high hysteria: "Murder! The exploiters, the bloodsuckers, the manufacturers. . . . Pay your dues. . . . Down with the capitalists! Hurrah!" Once the crisis, whatever particular crisis it was, had died down the workers dropped out of the union and the union itself went back to sleep.

Perhaps tonight would be the same story all over again, hysteria followed by hibernation. Yet there was something in the atmosphere that said otherwise. The shirtwaist workers spoke in hushed voices, impressed by the size of the crowd. Things were going to change; they felt this in their bones. Were they to be ground down forever by the bosses? No, there was change in the air and on people's faces.

Some Italians had come, and a few of the "Americans," while the men were there in full force, the cutters, pressers, and shirtwaist designers, clothed in their hats and their dignity. All were huddled together under the low ceiling of a pillared room in a place called Cooper Union, where Abraham Lincoln once gave a speech. Knowing this, that Lincoln who freed the slaves had spoken in this room, gave added importance to the evening.

Certainly the speakers on the platform looked important. One was Samuel Gompers, his presence proclaimed in advance by screaming headlines throughout the Yiddish press. Jacob Panken was there, and Meyer London, both prominent members of the Socialist party. Most ILGWU members were socialists, as was much of the Lower East Side. Those who had lived under Russian tyranny seemed to have taken socialism in with their mothers' milk.

Although there were people calling themselves

socialists who were also radicals, believers in rev-
olution, leaders of the ILGWU were moderates,
if not actually conservative. Equality and social
justice were their themes — competition to be replaced by cooperation, profit-seeking with social
service. Patience would be required to reach
these goals, a slow progression of carefully
thought-out steps.

Mary Dreier was there as well, the only
woman scheduled to speak, her face tense and serious, and scholarly Benjamin Feigenbaum, who
would serve as chairman. The audience stole
glances at them while waiting for the evening's
events to unfold; they chattered, out of nervous-
ness, and because they'd never imagined they
could do what they were doing, attending a union
meeting, one that might call for a general strike.

On the platform the speakers waited for silence. The chairman waited. So many people in a
state of high excitement took a long time to come
to order, but at last the speeches began. Most
were in Yiddish. An expressive language, by
turns humorous and deeply passionate, laced
with irony, capable of high drama followed by
homely proverbs, it has the power to call forth
laughter as readily as tears, often both together.

Yet the speeches that evening were dull and
heavy with caution. Nobody wanted the shirt-

waist girls to suffer, they said, and a general
strike would mean suffering. It would mean
hunger, repeated arrests, even jail, they said, so
don't rush into things, use due deliberation, be
sober in your decisions, and they said this over
and over. It was the sincere belief of the union
men that women and girls needed to be led, just
as sheep and cattle did. This was part of the nat-
ural order of things, part of the Constitution itself, which established the right of men to vote
and to lead.

There were people, suffragists, who held other
beliefs. For the past sixty years they had been demanding votes for women, but whenever they
brought their petitions before Congress it was explained most patiently, and with the exquisite
courtesy due to the gentler sex, that politics was a
filthy business. Women were pure, motherhood a
sacred calling, therefore they must be protected
from politics, and in any case real women did not
want the vote. Who would care for the children
when they went to the polling places?

But if there were any suffragists in the hall that
evening they remained silent. One after another
the leaders advised moderation, as the girls moved
restlessly in their seats. Moderation was not what
they had come for, even Mary Dreier had little to
offer, and they wondered how long they'd been

shut up in this airless place, elbow to elbow, while being talked at. Two hours? Forever?

Then Jacob Panken rose to speak, and before he could open his mouth a young woman in the front of the hall jumped to her feet. "I want to say a few words," she announced. The crowd buzzed. People had recognized Clara Lemlich.

Somebody shouted, "Get up on the platform!"

Other voices joined in, "Yes, get up on the platform." She ran toward it, and they lifted her up and set her there among the dignitaries. Workers who'd been bored and sleepy only a few minutes earlier were eager to hear what one of their own had to say.

Some of the speakers expressed annoyance, however, pointing out that this person was not on the program. Chairman Feigenbaum retorted that she had every right to speak, being a worker and a union member.

So Clara Lemlich threw back her head, drew herself up to her full height, and cried out in Yiddish that reached to the farthest corners of the room: "I have listened to all the speeches, and I have no further patience for talk. I, too, have worked and suffered, and I am tired of talk. I move that we go on general strike. Now!"

A contagion of excitement swept the hall. People screamed — men, women, teenagers, stamping their feet, waving hats and handkerchiefs and canes in a tumult of approval that lasted five minutes, and when there was a moment of quiet the chairman asked for someone to second the resolution, and once more the assembly erupted, everyone seconding the motion.

Feigenbaum himself was so carried away by the outburst that he sprang to Clara Lemlich's side and thrust her right arm in the air. "Do you mean it in good faith?" he shouted. "Will you take the old Hebrew oath?"

Three thousand arms shot up as three thousand people yelled in unison: "If I turn traitor to the cause I now pledge, may this hand wither from the arm I raise!"

The speeches that followed were hardly heard. Everything after Clara Lemlich was an anticlimax. When the hall emptied later on people were still talking about the sensation she caused — a girl, a worker like themselves, who knew little English and nevertheless took over a meeting of thousands by saying aloud what they had in their hearts.

In the street outside they met the overflow from nearby halls, who had heard about the progress of the meeting by messenger. People drew into little groups to talk it over, shivering in the cold night air; few owned winter clothing, but they wrapped themselves tightly in their thin jackets while discussing in three languages Clara Lemlich and the strike.

Tomorrow they would be picketing. What would that be like, to be outdoors in the middle of the week, not working, not earning? Light from the street lamps fell on their hats and shadowed their faces as they expressed their fears about tomorrow. Italian girls, who always came to work escorted by parents or brothers, wondered if those guardians of virtue would permit them to stand on the street. Jewish girls, whose parents depended on their earnings, wondered what the family would say to an empty pay envelope, just as those who had come on their own and lived on their own wondered what they'd be eating, where they'd find money for rent.

The thugs would be there, so would the Irish policemen who carried nightsticks and used them, and arrests would be made. Any one of them might land in jail, which could taint her forever — who'd want to marry a known jailbird?

These were the things they talked about as they shivered under the street lamps, Jews, Italians, and Americans, in their high-button shoes, and the white shirtwaists they ironed at night with irons heated on the cookstove — tomorrow, and what it would bring. Even those who'd already lost the desire to strike knew they could not back out. Having sworn a sacred oath before God and their fellow workers, they had no way out.

Whatever lay ahead it was sure to be dangerous, and this knowledge both frightened and elated them, promising to turn them overnight into adults.

5

ON THE STREETS

Everyone reported for work the morning after the strike vote. Those who had taken the oath, as well as those who had only heard about it — and so many had heard that the news must have traveled by telepathy — waited uncertainly by their machines with hats and coats on.

As one worker remembered it, "Well, so we stayed whispering, and no one knowing what the other would do, not making up our minds, for two hours. Then I started to get up. And at just the same minute all — we all got up together, in one second. No one after the other; no one before. And when I saw it — that time — oh, it excites me so yet, I can hardly talk about it. So we all stood up, and all walked out together. And already out on the sidewalk in front the policemen stood with the clubs. One of them said, 'If you don't behave, you'll get this on your head.' And he shook his club at me.

"We hardly knew where to go — what to do next. But one of the American girls, who knew how to telephone, called up the Women's Trade Union League, and they told us all to come to a big hall a few blocks away."

They set off for the hall then, Clinton Hall, chosen as strike headquarters. But it was no easy matter to get there, for the streets were almost impassable. They had been taken over by a cheering, singing, gesticulating army of workers. In fact the entire East Side had become one seething mass of humanity that clogged the sidewalks and spilled out into the cobblestoned gutters.

Traffic, both horses and autos, had been stopped cold, and some two hundred police reserves and plainclothesmen had been called out to maintain order. It seemed the army might at any moment erupt into the rest of Manhattan, invading Wall Street and the Bowery. By ten o'clock 15,000 workers had left their machines. By nightfall, 25,000. Within the next few days the number rose to nearly 30,000, and it included some cutters, pressers, and finishers. Reporters marveled. One union official said, "I shall never again see such a sight."

Pauline Newman recalled the feelings of the workers: "I can see the young people, mostly women, walking down and not caring what might happen. The spirit, I think the spirit of a conqueror, led them on. They didn't know what was in store for them, didn't really think of the hunger, cold, loneliness, and what could happen to them. They didn't care on that particular day; that was their day."

Those who reached Clinton Hall, and were able to battle their way inside, put down $1.50 for union membership, payable in ten-cent installments. But the building could not contain these thousands. Some workers milled about aimlessly and then went home, others spent the day packed into streets near the building, still cheering and singing, still high with that thrilling sensation of having taken over the city.

The officials of Local 25 were now prisoners within their little room, pinned in place by the multitude that demanded to sign up, pay dues, and start picketing at once. After three exhausting days the men threw up their hands and told Mary Dreier she was in charge now. From that moment on, union officials would negotiate with the owners, leaving the daily conduct of the strike up to the League and the workers themselves.

The League, like Local 25, had expected a turnout of four or five thousand. They were bowled over by this army, utterly unprepared for it. They had organized strikes in the garment trade, small ones, usually confined to a single shop, but never before had they undertaken something on so vast a scale. They might fail, might be laughed at by the whole of New York as well as John Dyche and the ILGWU men, and all the same they knew this was the challenge they'd been hoping for — their chance to show the world they were more than highbrow butters-in, just as the shirtwaist makers were more than irresponsible little girls.

Twenty-four halls were rented all over the Lower East Side. Each shop was to have its own meeting room, with separate rooms for Yiddish, Italian, and English groups wherever possible.

Delegates would be elected from each of the shops, to bring the workers' demands to a central strike committee. Speakers would have to be found to report the progress of the strike back to the workers, those speakers fluent in Yiddish, English, or Italian. A strike fund would have to be raised, an information bureau set up where strikers could register for relief, or for help with legal and personal problems. Publicity was another vital need — photos and eyewitness accounts of workers on the picket lines being harassed by gorillas and police. The picket lines themselves would have to be organized.

In other words, the League had agreed to build a large and complex machine, to fit all its parts together, then set the whole in motion although they had never seen such a machine. Nobody had, since this was the first "general strike" in the garment trades, also the largest strike of women workers ever known in the United States until that moment.

Yet within the next few days the machine came creakily to life. Several labor groups pitched in, so did the New York Women's Committee of the Socialist party, the Bakers' Union lent a hall, Litzin's Theater opened its doors for mass meetings during the daytime, and order of a sort was restored to Clinton Hall, although the streets nearby remained chaotic.

A reporter for *Collier's* magazine saw masses of young people milling about there as if on holiday. It was "a scene of gaiety and flirtation," she said, "the girls elaborately dressed, their hair-does . . . towering." There was no room to march, yet from time to time spontaneous marches broke out. At one point word spread through the crowd that five hundred cutters had joined the union, and nine were from Triangle. This news met with cheers, wild applause, some girls linking arms and trying to dance.

Once inside Clinton Hall, the writer found a

different climate. At the end of a swarming corridor a fortification had been set up, made of desks and tables; this was the League's information bureau, where scores of confused, excited workers waited to register for the union. Heavily bearded old men pushed through the crowd selling apples and pretzels from baskets. Phones rang constantly — "Send a speaker quick, right now," someone implored, "the girls are here and they don't want to wait." The caller gave the address of one of the overflow halls.

Another call, from a different address: "Hurry up a speaker in Italian." The woman who took the call shook her head; there wasn't a single Italian organizer in the ILGWU.

Hordes of employers were there as well, the owners of small shops who were unable to afford even a few days' idleness. They would do anything, they said, sign anything, agree to anything. A blackboard beside the desks listed firms that had settled with the union and were ready to hire their workers back, and each of the owners was anxious to see his name on that board.

League women came and went, usually at a run. Some were "ladies," like Mary Dreier, others were worker-members, like Rose Schneiderman, a former cap maker, and Leonora O'Reilly, who had started work in a collar factory at the age of

eleven. Another League member, Rose Pastor
Stokes, known as the red Yiddish Cinderella,
used to work in a cigar factory. When she became
engaged to the son of a millionaire — they had
met at a settlement house — front page headlines
in the *New York Times* announced *J. G. Phelps
Stokes to Wed Young Jewess.* At strike headquarters
Mrs. Stokes delivered fiery speeches about free-
ing workers from the shackles of the bosses.

Beyond the entryway, behind the comings and
goings of employers and League leaders, the real
business of the shirtwaist strike went on in the
small, bare, unheated rooms where shop meetings
were held. Their purpose was to decide what concessions the workers wanted from the owners,
and in order to decide they would have to learn
what was possible, or likely, when to give way
and when to stand fast. They would also have to
conduct their meetings according to parliamen-
tary procedure, then elect and instruct delegates.
And at this point most of them knew nothing, not
even how to picket.

So the shop meetings became classrooms, with
League members, union officers, or friends of the
union serving as volunteer teachers. Labor history was taught, and the principles of unionism,
along with Robert's Rules of Order, what a union
or closed shop was, how to avoid arrest on the

picket lines, what to do if arrested, and the meaning of the word "solidarity," all of which the union
men knew by heart and had always known, apparently from childhood.

Many were eloquent speakers, like Morris
Hillquit, one of the leaders of the Socialist party,
who explained why manufacturers opposed the
union: "They like you individually," he said.
"They say to each of you that you are lovable, but
when you, lovable girls, are formed into a bunch
of lovable girls then you cease to be lovable."

He described how women were forced to com-
pete with their own brothers, husbands, and fathers, by doing the same work at a lower wage
because of their unorganized condition. "Your
work is no fun and your strike is no joke, and
shame on the newspapers who make light of it because you happen to be girls."

Lectures were given round the clock by the
volunteer teachers, some speaking thirteen or
fourteen times a day in the cheerless rooms of the
rented halls. Clara Lemlich remembered talking
nonstop for what seemed like days at a time; the
shirtwaist strike had become her life. The workers drank in their lessons, taking them so fer-
vently to heart that those opening days of the
strike had the spirit of revival meetings, the
workers new converts to some soul-saving reli-

gion. They would win, they had only to stick together and wait it out. What a wonderful thing
the union was. They loved it, they gave themselves to it, clasping it to their bosoms, putting all
their faith in it and in one another.

The shop meetings had their own stories to tell,
stories of leaders who sprang up out of nowhere.
Girls and women who had never thought of
themselves as remarkable stepped forward to
take charge wherever needed, amazing everyone,
including themselves. Some were experienced
and well paid, with less cause to complain than
the general mass of workers, and it was exactly
this that inspired them. "It touched their sense of
sympathy," one observer explained, "and infused
into the strike the spirit of a great altruism."
There was a feeling that everyone was working
for her neighbor and that "the strong were cham-
pioning the cause of the weak."

Esther Lobetkin, a recent immigrant, became
chairman of her Yiddish-speaking group, marching with the strikers by day, then rushing to Clinton Hall to report and attend meetings until the
small hours of the morning. A sandwich at mid-
night and an hour of sleep were all she seemed to
need. Although she was arrested time and again,
she never failed to yell from the back of the patrol
wagon, "Do not lose courage! We'll win yet!"

A Miss Reisen, another Yiddish speaker, took command of a roomful of Italian strikers when no one else was willing to. Almost daily, someone would jump up and offer to lead the rest back to work, and Miss Reisen, who knew no Italian, would guess what was said, and leap to the platform. Pleading with the workers to stay, she was met with insults and abuse, yet many did stay. The Italians were always on the brink of desertion; so were the "Americans," partly because the union men, mostly Russian intellectuals, tended to browbeat them.

The picketers were the combat troops, the foot soldiers who went daily into battle. Within days of the strike call, the Association of Waist and Dress Manufacturers of New York — formed and dominated by the largest firms — declared open war against the union. They urged small owners who had already made settlements to repudiate them. A trade agreement with the union "was not worth the paper it was written on." New workers were hired, and reinforcements for the ranks of gorillas. They used their fists routinely against girl strikers, and, just as routinely, police hauled the strikers away for disorderly conduct. Each time the story was different, but the results were always the same — arrests, the patrol wagon, fines or jail sentences, and the thugs released. Yet the picket lines went out each day, battle-ready.

Reporters from the city's daily newspapers were always on hand now; the strike was their assigned beat, almost every issue carrying some mention of it, especially the *New York Call* and the *Forward*, both active supporters. The *Times* seemed to waver, while William Randolph Hearst's New York *Evening Journal* was consistently friendly. Dailies in other major cities brought strike news to thousands of distant homes, and national magazines, above all those intended for women, carried articles in a sentimental vein, with the strikers invariably shown as soulfully pale, dark-eyed, and sensitive.

Soon women's groups throughout the country were drawn to the side of the workers, reformers moved to tears by stories of teenaged girls who were beaten by professional thugs, and jailed by corrupt judges. It was like Russia, people said, where Cossacks terrorized and murdered Jews.

Yet what they wanted was modest enough: a fifty-two-hour week with extra pay for overtime, an end to the fines and petty tyrannies, and a living wage. These were the demands that were hammered out by the shop groups behind the closed doors of the meeting halls. The officers of Local 25 sent them on to the owners — along with one more demand, recognition of the union. This came to mean the "closed shop." Only union members can work in a closed shop, since the only way to set uniform wages and standards is to have the union do it; otherwise employers would always try to undercut one another. And the union can standardize the industry only when it controls the supply of labor through the union shop.

Workers and leaders alike believed the manufacturers' association was sure to give in. It might take two weeks, possibly as much as three. But it would happen. Some fifty owners of small shops had already agreed to all union demands, even the closed shop, and almost half the original 30,000 were back at work. How could it not happen?

But for the time being, the big owners and their followers refused to budge. With unlimited financial resources and the continued support of police and judges, they were convinced that time was on their side — time and the weather.

Many of the workers were still penniless from the dull summer season, and had never bought warm clothes. They wore short little jackets or sweaters, their best shirtwaists, and their largest hats, those with the most elaborate decorations. They thought of themselves as representing their union to the rest of the world, therefore a good appearance was important. So they marched in twos and threes, shivering, and holding their signs aloft. Everywhere in the garment district, by the front gates of little shops and big ones, picketers marched and sang. "O Dubinushka," they sang, and "Tortured and Enslaved," and other Russian folk and revolutionary airs. Icy rains poured down on them, some were in danger of frostbite — a winter of record-breaking cold had already begun — but there they were and there they stayed.

The union men were amazed. "There never was anything like it," one ILGWU official declared. "An equal number of men never would hold together under what these girls are enduring."

6

"COLLEGE GIRLS"

A week into the strike, and the *Call* was reporting morale even higher than before. An all-day mass meeting in support of the strike, planned for November 30, promised speakers from such male strongholds as the Rockdrillers and Tool Sharpeners' Union, the Dockbuilders, the Hod-Carriers, the Rockmen and Excavators, the Electricians, and the Cigar-Packers. Shop meetings throughout the East Side were jammed with cheering, enthusiastic workers. Small employers continued their parade into Clinton Hall, where they settled with the union, "and everywhere the watchword was — what some have achieved all can win."

Yet unless this victory took place overnight they were going to need substantial transfusions of money. The ILGWU had only a limited strike fund and much of it went to paying fines. Thanks to contributions from the League, the *Call,* the *Forward,* and other supporters, small stipends were offered for living expenses — three dollars a week for workers with dependents, $1.50 for those without. Some workers refused to take anything at all, but with so many thousands of unemployed even these small sums added up. ILGWU officials decided on a series of fund-raising talks.

Pauline Newman, then nineteen years old, was instructed to start a tour of New York State on half-a-day's notice: "I was called by Secretary John Dyche and he told me, 'You are going to Buffalo tonight.' I told him I had never been out of town in my entire life and didn't even own a suitcase. 'You can have mine,' he said." He brought her the suitcase and took her to the train, where he handed her a one-way ticket to Buffalo. How was she to continue the tour? By raising money, he said. "'Remember, we have no money.'"

Rose Schneiderman was assigned to New England. Several years older than her friend Pauline Newman, already a seasoned organizer and destined to become one of the most remarkable figures in American labor, she was usually referred to as "little Rose Schneiderman," because she was no more than four-and-a-half feet tall, weighing about ninety pounds, the whole topped by a head of brilliant red hair.

She had been born in Russian Poland, the el-

dest child of an Orthodox Jewish family that
came to America when Rose was eight. Her father died, leaving her mother with four small children and another on the way. For a time they
lived on charity and whatever their mother could
earn by sewing, but then the mother grew desperate, and in her desperation sent Rose and a
younger brother to an orphanage, where at least
they'd be clothed and fed.

After the family was reunited, Rose left school
at the age of thirteen to work as a department
store "cash-girl," bringing in two dollars for a
sixty-four-hour week. At sixteen, she took a bet-
ter-paying job making cap-linings, in spite of her
mother's objections that factory work was not
genteel. Four years later she launched her union
career; joining with two other young women, she
organized their shop and led the workers out on
strike. As Mary Dreier recalled, "They had a revolutionary spirit, knew hardship and dared the
impossible. When they won, they had a banquet,
the first of its kind, costing the great sum of
twenty-five cents a plate!"

Rose Schneiderman had become a League
member in 1905 in order to dedicate her life to
working women. Her mother told her this was
unwise, that if she married the union she would

never get a husband. The duty of a Jewish daughter was to marry and beget, and she was a dutiful daughter, but she had set her feet on a certain path, and in the course of a long life never swerved from it.

In union halls, or mounted on a soapbox in the street, she was able to tell women workers hard truths about the fate of unorganized female labor, and to do it in ways that people like Mary Dreier could not, since they had never lived those truths. "If you think you will be a grand lady after you leave the factory and are married to the working-man you are sadly mistaken," she said, "for you will have to work yourself to death."

The streetcorner talks were usually in Yiddish, but Rose Schneiderman was equally effective in English. Touring New England, lecturing at women's colleges and parlor meetings of alumnae, she raised not only money but something even more valuable, the political consciousness of young women.

Fresh faces began appearing on the picket lines — youthful faces, often under fur hats. Some came because they'd heard Rose Schneiderman speak, others were friends of League women, or even League members themselves. As recent graduates of elite schools like Vassar, Wellesley, and Bryn Mawr, they were lumped together by journalists into a single category, the "college girls." Newspapers found them fascinating, funny, and above all, remarkable.

In that era, when few Americans received even a high school diploma, women who went to college were sometimes a source of amusement, always a novelty. The young women who joined the picket lines now were novel in other ways, for most had independent incomes, in some cases amounting to millions. Children of an exceptionally privileged class, they spoke its language and wore its clothes, typically imported from abroad, and shared its pastimes — opera, concerts, travel to Europe — and in the garment district they were as alien as visitors from another planet.

Like those who join the Peace Corps today, they had come out of idealism, but also to experience a foreign culture, the world of the East Side with its thugs and gangs and prostitutes. The older League women were also college graduates, including a few who were lawyers or physicians, but there was nothing girlish about them. And they had not come in search of adventure. They were reformers, serious-minded people who thought of themselves as "social housekeepers." The college girls, on the other hand, were still in their early twenties. High-spirited, eager for a

challenge, they reached out to their younger sisters, the shirtwaist makers.

This claim of instant kinship was seized upon
by the newspapers. According to a long story in
the *Times*, "It was a sort of 'you-a-girl-and-me-a-
girl' spirit that started it. The factory girl makes
shirtwaists and the college girl wears them, and
when they first walked Broadway arm in arm as
pickets in the big shirtwaist strike that is now on,
they both wore the garment of contention. . . .
For once the factory girl and the college girl are
making a fight together."

One of the most conspicuous was Inez Milholland, who had graduated that year from Vassar
and planned to go on to law school, then devote
her life to reform causes. She was tall, athletic,
mischievous, beautiful, and held such radical
opinions as a belief in free love, which she did
not hesitate to express. While at Vassar she had
enrolled two-thirds of her fellow students in a
suffrage organization, and when two leading suffragists visited the campus, she defied a college
ban by calling a meeting in a nearby cemetery.
Inez Milholland brought her boyfriends to the
Lower East Side. One was arrested briefly when
she was; another, the young editor of a struggling
radical magazine, helped plan strategy for the
strike.

Carola Woerishoffer was a Bryn Mawr graduate and the heiress to a railroad fortune, so deeply interested in the lives of working women that she had taken a summer job in a New York steam laundry. There she spent four months bent over tubs of boiling wash, working in temperatures that often reached 100 degrees. She said she wanted to see what it was like to live on what she could earn without skills, using just her two hands.

Elsie Cole, also from Vassar, became known as "that woman that talks," because of her eloquence on the picket line. Factory owners found she could make a full-fledged argument and win her point while they were still struggling for words. Elsie Cole was arrested three times, after which nobody bothered to arrest her.

Violet Pike, another Vassar graduate, was described by an observer as "dainty little Violet . . . her hands deep in her pockets, her beaver hat a bit to the side and an angelic smile on her red lips. . . . I must say she's the bravest of the brave, Violet is." Stopping one morning to speak to a strange worker, a possible strikebreaker, she was told by the policeman to move on. "I will when I'm through," she said. "You can arrest me if you want." To this the officer retorted, "Oh, you uptown scum!"

Emily Taft, an undergraduate at Bryn Mawr

and the daughter of President Taft, arrived one afternoon for a brief visit and promised to tell her father about the brave shirtwaist strikers. Others raised money for the strike fund, either from their own pockets or by speech-making, and still others, like Inez Milholland, volunteered legal advice. But they were most valuable on the picket line, giving heart to the strikers, restraining them when they were in danger of arrest, talking back for them to bosses or police or strikebreakers. The college girl could afford to talk back, having no fear of the owner, the police force, or even the courts. Such is the power of an independent income.

Sometimes a crowd would form at the factory gate. There would be men in the crowd who jostled and pushed, hoping to shove the pickets into the gutter, but if the pickets shoved back they could be arrested. When the workers came out at quitting time they might hurl insults at the pickets, who would be tempted to yell insults of their own, but if they used the word "scab," for this, too, they could be arrested. If a strikebreaker slapped a picket that was one thing, but if the picketer slapped the strikebreaker it became assault, disorderly conduct, or whatever the officer on the beat cared to call it. And as the *Times* points out, in each case it was up to the college girl to urge restraint, with the picket line occasionally turning on her, asking what on earth they were supposed to do: "They push us off the sidewalk and we can't push them! They holler names and we can't even call 'scab,' what can we do?"

The *Times* reporter pictures the college girl confronting the factory owner at the end of the day, when he waits to have a word with her, possibly "out of mere curiosity. . . . He is not a coward. He is not mean. Perhaps he has only been a boss two years and was a union man himself. At any rate, he has his ideas, and he can express them. The volunteer picket must know her case to the letter, and be crafty at handling it, or she will have no weight with the boss. . . . It is significantly not this man's shop alone, or this strike, which is the matter of contention — it is the whole woman movement, or the labor movement, about which, as the boss puts it, 'you women that ain't got anything to do think it's stylish to butt in.'"

College girls rode in the patrol wagon, and stood by in night court, where the strikers sometimes went to pieces. Young, inexperienced, ill-at-ease with the English language and trembling before a judge, they were often unable to speak up for themselves, and the college girls did it for them.

At other times there was little they could do,
since the strikers resisted anything that smacked
of charity. Again the source is the *Times:* "One girl
of fifteen went hungry for two days before she
whispered her trouble to one of the other girls.
She had three (younger) children to support, a
sick mother and a blind father. She ate very little
from the first, because she knew that her money
would not last long and she wanted to stay out
two weeks, at least. But when the two weeks
were up . . . her courage began to fail. She was
eating less and less every day. . . . It was in a moment of weakness that she told the leader of her
shop strike just how she was situated. The leader
could get but $3 that week from the union, so the
girls clubbed together and made up the amount to
finance her for another week. There are hundreds
of girls just like this. . . . Yet it is hard . . . to
make them see that taking the money is not taking charity."

This was what the "college girls" learned during the course of the strike, such information not
being available at Vassar or Bryn Mawr. The
shirtwaist makers loved them unashamedly, for
their courage, their friendship, and for the message they brought — that they, the workers, were
not alone. The rest of the world knew and cared

about them, including these glamorous young
women who never pulled rank, never suggested
they were smarter or better. As the *Times* said of
the college girl, "she has already become one
of the main factors in the fight, representing a
power of outside interference which may win or
lose the strike."

There was another important aspect to the
coming of the college girls. The shirtwaist strikers
never thought of themselves as militant femi-
nists — the phrase was unknown at the time —
neither did they believe they were ever likely
to become the equals of men. Yet the strike was
changing the ways they saw themselves and the
world.

Owners of factories were sufficiently afraid of
them that a small army of gorillas had been hired
to scare them off. Major newspapers recorded the
events of their daily lives. Women's magazines
carried stories that emphasized their altruism.
And now there were people like Inez Milholland
to whom they were sisters and comrades. Not
victims in need of pity, but fighters. Models of independent womanhood.

All this was heady stuff. It stiffened the spines
of the shirtwaist strikers and made them proud of
being exactly what they were — workers, immi-

grants, "greenhorns." Meanwhile, it seemed as if the whole of New York had fallen in love with them. Charles K. Harris wrote a song, "Heaven Will Protect the Working Girl," and it was on everyone's lips.

7

THE MINK BRIGADE

Early in December some ten thousand workers assembled at the Bowery. Carrying banners that read PEACEFUL PICKETING IS THE RIGHT OF EVERY WOMAN, they proceeded four abreast in a silent and solemn march toward City Hall. A squad of mounted police led the parade, police guarded the sides and rear, reporters swarmed behind.

At City Hall a committee of three League women, and three strikers who had been brutally beaten on the picket line, were received with grave courtesy by Mayor George McClellan. He bowed several times, he accepted their petition, a protest against police abuse, and listened attentively to their descriptions of two hundred arrests made in the past ten days alone. He was told that all those arrested had been insulted and mistreated by his "Cossacks."

The mayor listened with particular interest to a

girl named Yetta Ruth, whom the *Call* described as a very pretty seventeen-year-old with red cheeks and black eyes. She had been at work in her shop, she said, where she expressed sympathy with the strikers, for which the owner called policemen who dragged her to the West Twentieth Street police station. "The officer asked me with how many men I was living," she went on. Another officer called her a dirty socialist and anarchist; other things were said that she could not understand, but whose meaning she guessed at. She blushed while she spoke.

When all the speeches were done the mayor thanked the committee, promised to take the matter up with his police commissioner, and bowed them out. However, there were no results whatsoever from the meeting. Almost two weeks had passed since the start of the strike, but thugs and police continued to bully the strikers, magistrates favored the owners, and members of the manufacturers' association found ingenious ways to conduct business.

Many were sending their orders to factories in Philadelphia, who made the shirtwaists that were then marketed under the label of the New York firm. There was talk of the strike spreading to Philadelphia; taking no chances, Triangle opened

Interior of a sweatshop in New York City.

A family living in a Lower East Side tenement.

New York's Lower East Side in 1910.

Samuel Gompers speaking on the night the general strike is called.

Strikers volunteering for picket duty.

*A formal picture of Pauline Newman and Clara Lemlich,
after the strike.*

Headquarters of the Women's Trade Union League.

Picketers being taken to Jefferson Market Prison.

Picketers came from many different backgrounds.

Rose Pastor Stokes, a factory worker who married a millionaire.

Some of the determined strikers, spring 1910.

Rose Schneiderman dedicated her life to working women.

a plant of its own in Yonkers. They advertised for factory hands, claiming that shirtwaist makers ought to move there because living was cheaper. Other large New York plants hired Italians, or newly arrived Jewish immigrants, or else blacks, who had rarely been welcome in the garment district. So members of the owners' association saw no need to settle the strike. They were producing shirtwaists, they would sell them, and they refused to be dictated to by a union composed of children.

It was at this point that a formidable new ally appeared at strike headquarters, a large and stately matron, Mrs. O. H. P. Belmont, one of the leaders of New York society. "She loved a fight," according to the autobiography of her daughter, Consuelo Vanderbilt Balsan. "A born dictator, she dominated events about her. . . . If she admitted another point of view she never conceded it."

Mrs. Belmont's full name was Alva Erskine Smith Vanderbilt Belmont, and the name summarizes the personal history that brought her to the Lower East Side. Born in Mobile, Alabama, where local legend had it that the Smiths were never accepted by "old Mobile" society, she had come to Manhattan with her family in the 1870s. For a time they took in boarders.

Alva Smith, a plain-looking young person of no particular importance, managed nevertheless to marry William Kissam Vanderbilt, a grandson of the Cornelius Vanderbilt who founded the family fortune. Although the wedding was the greatest social event of the season, the inner circle of old New York society refused to accept these Vanderbilts, however rich. Old New York society was personified by Mrs. William B. Astor. She did not recognize the Vanderbilts, and would not pay a formal call on the new Mrs. Vanderbilt, a simple gesture consisting of nothing more than driving up to the front door and giving a calling card to the servant who opened the door.

Therefore Mrs. Vanderbilt resolved to bludgeon her way into old New York society. She hired a fashionable architect, and together they created a three-million-dollar château on Fifth Avenue, as well as a mansion in Newport inspired by the Grand Trianon in Versailles. New York society continued to ignore her, however, just as Mobile society had ignored Alva Smith.

Rising to the challenge, Mrs. Vanderbilt then sent out invitations to a costume ball. It was to be an extravagant entertainment, and the younger set ordered their costumes and rehearsed their dances, even Mrs. Astor's adolescent daughter, who had not been invited. Alva Vanderbilt, the born dictator, waited. Mrs. Astor, who was a loving mother, had no choice but to pay the call. It happened that both women came to the ball dressed as Venetian princesses, with Mrs. Astor somewhat more splendid since she wore the Astor jewels. But Mrs. Vanderbilt was now an acknowledged member of New York society.

Not even her suit for divorce, accusing her husband of adultery, could shake this position once she had attained it. One year later the former Mrs. Vanderbilt became Mrs. Oliver Hazard Perry Belmont. Her new husband was the son of a millionaire banker.

At much the same time she married off her nineteen-year-old daughter, not to the young lawyer Consuelo loved, but to Charles Richard John Spencer-Churchill, 9th Duke of Marlborough. Such marriages were not uncommon at the time; titled European families were glad to be joined to American fortunes. But in this case the bride was so reluctant that it had to be done almost forcibly. "I have always had absolute power over my daughter," Mrs. Belmont said, years later. "I, therefore, did not beg, but ordered her to marry the Duke."

When Oliver Belmont died in 1908, this extra-

ordinary woman found herself more or less at
loose ends. Fifty-six years old, with the tempera-
ment of a field marshal, she needed troops to
command and a cause to fight for. Overnight, to
the stunned wonderment of her friends, she
transformed herself into a suffragist.

Leasing an entire floor of a Fifth Avenue building as headquarters for an established suffrage
organization, she also set up one of her own, the
Political Equality Association. When the press
was invited to view the premises, they asked who
would be the officers of the new organization.
Mrs. Belmont replied there would be only one:
herself.

It was her next move that brought her into the
strike community. Mrs. Belmont, that specialist
in magnificent gestures, rented the New York
Hippodrome for a rally in support of the strikers.
It was newly built and enormous, made to accom-
modate an audience of many thousands, and at
Clinton Hall the rally was all people could talk
about. "It is rather strange, her offering to pay for
the big place," one observer remarked. "I wonder
what made her do it. . . . The papers say that
Mrs. Belmont is worth millions; that each of her
hats and suits is worth hundreds of dollars. . . .
I'm anxious to have a look at her tomorrow."

On the day itself, the same observer continued, "It did my heart good to see how happy every one of our girls looked. . . . It is really a wonderful feeling that comes over one when a body finds itself surrounded by thousands of people all assembled for the same purpose, breathing the same hopes and thinking the same thoughts — it's like an immense giant born for the purpose of doing justice to all."

The stage was done up as if for a suffrage rally. Blue-and-white flags carried such messages as, WE DEMAND EQUAL PAY FOR EQUAL WORK, and GIVE WOMEN THE PROTECTION OF THE VOTE. Figures displayed the relative pay of men and women teachers in city schools, as well as the miserable wages of women workers in wig-making, and white goods (the manufacture of household linen), and in commercial laundries where they worked stripped to the waist over vats of boiling water.

Fashionable people filled the boxes. In the audience workers and socialists found themselves side by side with men and women so rich they could hardly count their wealth — fighters for industrial justice united with fighters for civil rights. Prominent clergymen spoke, among them the Rev. Mr. Alexander Irving, who told the strikers the manufacturers wanted to keep them from doing the only thing worth doing. "Get your union," he said, "fight for it to the last."

Rose Pastor Stokes spoke, and Leonora O'Reilly, with tears streaming down her face. "I am here by the right of three generations of shirt-makers," she said, "my mother's mother having sung the song of the shirt when the potatoes went out in Ireland." A speech was given in Italian by a labor organizer named Publio Mazella, who pointed out that this was the first time in the history of the Italian labor movement in New York that an Italian had been invited to address such a meeting.

Mrs. Belmont, who was not on the platform but in a private box, had invited the mayor, the district attorney, and other city officials to share it with her. They told her they were otherwise engaged, and in any case labor matters did not interest them, and while these letters were being read aloud by the chairman the audience hissed in unison. Once the rally was over the workers walked twenty blocks back to the Lower East Side, still unsure about Mrs. Belmont's motives.

The *Times* was equally unsure. Pushing international news to the background, they gave the rally their front-page lead: "Socialism, unionism, woman suffrage and what seemed to be something like anarchism were poured into the ears of fully eight thousand persons to attend the mass meeting held there by Mrs. O. H. P. Belmont." Apparently they suspected her of dangerously radical tendencies.

That same day, the fifth of December, saw the first serious attempt to settle the strike. Labor leaders addressed letters to Local 25 and to the owners' association, asking if the two parties would agree to arbitration. If they did, a board of six — two representing the workers, two representing employers, and two others chosen by these four — would examine the dispute from all sides and offer a solution. On the following day the owners accepted this offer of arbitration.

But from the first it was clear that the effort was doomed to failure. The labor people had demanded recognition of the union as a precondition, yet the owners flatly refused. The labor people then agreed to proceed with arbitration anyhow, but once the group of six got together, the owners would not allow the arbitrators even to consider this matter of union recognition. There were further attempts at bringing the two sides together, and further stonewalling on the part of the owners.

On the thirteenth of December, in pouring rain, hundreds of strikers waited at Grand Central Palace two hours before its doors opened, to hear what progress had been made. Other hundreds followed, until there were 7,500 in all. According to a woman who attended the rally: "Earnestly, without any flourishes, the lawyer told us just what reply he had received. . . . They didn't want to make any settlement . . . they don't want to yield one jot as far as the union is concerned."

The lawyer further pointed out that the owners had a large backlog of orders on hand, on which they hoped to make a good deal of money, and as this could not be done without the help of the workers, they were sure to change their minds in time. At this the strikers jumped to their feet. There were cheers, foot-stomping, cries of, "We stand by the union until we die!"

When the hall was quiet again, Rose Schneiderman got up to remind them that it was "worthwhile to starve a year in order to gain recognition of the union." She announced a gift of $1,525 from Mrs. Belmont and her friends, people she privately called "the mink brigade." There were more cheers and yells. But the voices were shrill and hoarse, many of the girls being too hungry to yell naturally. Outside, the rain continued to pour down, and most had to get carfare home from the union, not having even ten cents to their names.

In neighborhood pawnshops the bits of jewelry worn by young girls were beginning to show up — bracelets, earrings, little pins. How else was a penniless worker to get to strike headquarters on a rainy day, or buy a meal from a push-cart?

8

THE TOMBS

Clinton Hall, once filled with laughter and high hopes — where speakers had declared what a glorious thing this fight was, and the workers in turn had embraced the union like a sweetheart — was quiet now. They were starting the fourth week of the strike. According to the *Times*, "They are coming to see that they are facing something terribly real and terribly hard. . . . They know that the powerful union, which they idealized too much in the beginning, hasn't given them immediately what they want immediately . . . all those still out of work now know that striking isn't a matter of pretty words . . . but hard reality — hard times."

Certainly the weather was hard, an implacable enemy that never let up, numbing hands, feet, faces. Some strikers went straight from the picket line to the hospital with frostbite. Others came down with respiratory ailments. Almost everyone was hungry, and many were living on one meal a day.

The violence continued, even escalated. A woman striker was stabbed in the shoulder by a knife-wielding scab, a man slashed in the face by another. The *Call* began referring contemptuously to the thugs as "heroes." And in the courtroom, magistrates discovered a new and potent weapon — the workhouse on Blackwell's Island, a grim institution also known as the Tombs.

Judge Cornell explained his reasoning: "I find the girls guilty. It would be perfectly futile for me to fine them. Some charitable women would pay their fines. . . . I am going to commit them to the workhouse under the Cumulative Sentence Act, and there they will have an opportunity of thinking over what they have done."

The workhouse was meant for repeat offenders, such disturbers of the peace as habitual drunks, prostitutes, and drug addicts. Prisoners lived six to a cell, with a single bucket that remained overnight serving all six as their toilet. Rats scratched at the walls, and crawled under and across the cots. Days were spent scrubbing stone floors on hands and knees. Misbehavior was punished by confinement in the darkroom — "the so-much dreaded darkroom," as one reporter described it, "where a body remains strapped down to a pole in a pitch-dark corner and must keep moving the feet all the while to frighten the many rats away." There were hardened prisoners who demanded to know what teenaged girls were doing in such a place.

One of those who went was little Rose Perr, a fifteen-year-old so thin and small that she hardly looked more than ten. The workhouse uniform, made of some coarse material with stripes all around, was much too large for her, and so heavy it seemed to drag her to the ground; the sleeves trailed over her hands, the skirts had to be held up with safety pins.

The *Literary Digest* compared the hundreds of arrests, the fines, jail sentences, and five-day terms in the workhouse with the gentle treatment of men who took part in a chauffeurs' strike one year earlier. During five violent weeks, marked by bloody hand-to-hand combat between scabs and strikers that landed scores in the hospital, there were no jail sentences at all, and only a half dozen fines. What accounted for the difference? A group of chauffeurs put it very simply: "The girls haven't any vote."

The League drew up a set of rules for pick-eters, hoping to cut down on the number of ar-rests. They were told not to walk in groups of more than two or three. Not to stop the person they wanted to talk to, but walk alongside him. Not to get excited or shout when talking. Not to put a hand on the person they spoke to, or touch his sleeve, since that could be taken as a "technical assault." And if arrested in spite of obeying the rules they were to take down the policeman's number and give it to union officers.

Would it help? Probably not. Some workers reported being arrested simply for showing up on the picket line — "the boss has it in for me," they said.

At the same time it was clear that the manufacturers were suffering as well. Two people from Gross & Weiss went to strike headquarters in search of former employees. Come to a meeting, they told them, the firm will put out a barrel of beer. Others visited workers at home, promising to make individual settlements — never mind the union, they said, just come back, and we will forget you ever left.

In the words of the *Call,* "the unkindest cut of all, and the one that the bosses cannot understand, is the fact that the rich ladies, the customers, have expressed in unmistakable terms their sympathy with the strikers. . . . Many newspapermen were kept engaged for hours in the effort to make them believe that the manufacturers too have a side."

Meanwhile Rose Schneiderman continued her fund-raising lectures to churches and women's clubs all over the city. One evening she spoke in a theater, where a benefit performance was being given for one of the suffrage groups, and for days afterward letters poured into the League office from society women asking how they could help. One came from Anne Morgan, the youngest child of the banker John Pierpont Morgan. He was not the richest man in America, but it would be no exaggeration to say he was the most powerful figure in American business.

The historian Frederick Lewis Allen gives the following description: "This gruff, thundering, awe-inspiring man with the hideous red nose and the piercing eyes — this banker, promoter, churchman, art collector, yachtsman, and philanthropist — this inwardly shy, deeply religious, narrowly patrician, and boldly enterprising gentleman was no believer in competition. Morgan seemed to feel that the business machinery of America should be honestly and decently managed by a few of the best people, people like his friends and associates."

And Rose Schneiderman, with Anne Morgan's letter before her, understandably wondered aloud,

"What does the daughter of that capitalist want with us?"

What Miss Morgan wanted was to talk about the strike and how she, too, could share in it. Word of this development spread rapidly through the garment district. Employers hoped to intercept her before she made promises to the strikers. The strikers themselves were dazzled by the prospect of meeting her, of seeing her from close up, possibly shaking her hand. They knew her from the newspapers the way royalty is known; the family yacht, the homes in England and France, the dresses ordered ever since childhood in wholesale lots from the best fashion house in Paris — all were familiar to them. They tried to imagine what her father had to say on the subject, tried to picture that imperious man when he heard his child was coming to the Lower East Side to make common cause with factory workers.

The same question was on every journalist's mind. An intimate friend of the family told a reporter, "Mr. Morgan naturally has very different views from Anne, but he is a broadminded man and respects his daughter for thinking and acting for herself. . . . the story that he had angrily sworn to disinherit her for her avowed sympathy for the strikers is absolutely false."

Nobody believed a word of it. Some remem-

bered descriptions of Miss Morgan from the society pages in which she was said to be shy and
docile, active in church work. She had been
plump as a girl, almost stodgy-looking, with an
indecisive mouth. Surely her father was infuri-
ated by the change.

The woman who turned up at Clinton Hall was
thirty-seven years old now, no longer plump, certainly far from indecisive. Tall, dark-haired, surrounded by the smoke of her Turkish cigarettes,
she moved fast and spoke fast. Her voice was low
and slightly hoarse, and everything she said had a
directness. She was there to work, she told them.
She craved work, was addicted to it. Perhaps she
felt guilty for having been born to wealth. Perhaps she was rebelling against her all-powerful
father, whose piercing eyes and heavy eyebrows
she seemed to have inherited. Yet she said nothing about herself or her father; there was no
personal talk at all, just calm and disciplined
graciousness. She would start by joining the
League's executive board as a provisional member, she would march on a picket line, and after
that she would see for herself what needed doing.

Mrs. Belmont inspired awe, but Anne Morgan
was almost approachable. She shook hands with
everyone, spoke to everyone. And in mid-Decem-
ber she gave a luncheon at the Colony Club —

*The certificate that formally created the
International Ladies Garment Workers Union.*

Female factory workers at lunchtime.

Participants in a Ladies Garment Workers Parade.

Shirtwaist workers marching to City Hall in 1909.

Mrs. O.H.P. Belmont and her daughter Consuela Vanderbilt.

Anne Morgan helped raise money and support for the strikers.

Mary Dreier denounced unfair treatment of strikers by police.

Inez Milholland, a prominent suffragette.

The Triangle Shirtwaist Factory after the devastating fire.

Legendary labor agitator Mother Jones.

146 workers were killed in the Triangle Factory fire.

A page from the 1909 Sears, Roebuck and Company catalog.

the city's first social club for women, one she had
helped to found — so that its members could
meet some of the strikers and learn about their
cause.

On gilt chairs, in the club's sumptuous gymna-
sium, some 150 women representing the richest
people in the country came face to face with ten
shirtwaist workers. The room was filled with
flowers; the workers wondered how it was possible to find flowers in December. They wondered
at the music, the furs and jewels and clothing of
the women, the silver services set out on the tea
tables. "I couldn't help comparing it with the
breakfast I had this morning in Mrs. Bloom's
kitchen," one of the guests said later, "seven of us,
some standing, others sitting on a chair, a box or
washtub, each holding a roll and a cup of weak
coffee."

Clara Lemlich spoke in Yiddish, Rose Schneiderman acted as translator: "I could tell you,
ladies, how I spend my life and live on fifteen dollars, but I have no right to speak when there are
others who make three dollars a week."

An Italian girl who worked as a finisher said,
"Yes, I get four cents a dozen for waists. A priest
came to our shop and told us girls that if we
struck we should go — excuse me please,
ladies — to hell."

A girl who supported three younger children and her parents explained life on $3.50 a week: "My mother can't see good out of her eyes. That's all I've got to say. I am fifteen years old."

When Mary Dreier spoke, she told them the strike had given names to girls who were only numbers before — Jews and Italians who never knew each other's names. The fight had begun in earnest now, she said. It was simply a question of "which will win — the employers with plenty of money or the girls with none."

After that everyone had tea, rich sandwiches, fruit, and exquisite little cakes. While they ate, some of the workers felt they were being stared at, as if the society women, who had never before seen Jewish factory girls, were more curious than polite. They finished by donating $1,300 to the strike fund. Several of the millionairesses even joined the picket lines the next day.

Rich Women's Aid Gives Strikers Hope, reported the *Times. Shirtwaist Girls Sure of Victory Since Miss Morgan and Others Joined Their Cause*. The strike had crippled the industry, they said. One firm was forced into bankruptcy. "The girls, who had been overawed by the wealth and power of the employers, now feel that they have powerful friends of their own."

This was not entirely true. Emma Goldman —
political activist and radical, believer in free
speech and birth control and anarchism, meaning
the end of all government — spoke for many
when she told the *Literary Digest* she did not trust
rich women. "It is all very sentimental and fine
and kind for the ladies of the Colony Club to
come forward," she said, "but they can help the
girls better as a class by getting off their backs."
A few members of the League, as well as some of
the strikers, had all along held certain reserva-
tions about the "mink brigade," and the splendor
of the Colony Club only served to strengthen them.

However the millionairesses paid no attention
to the words of Red Emma, if indeed they were
aware of them. Mrs. Belmont did whatever she
liked; other points of view never interested her.
In her spare time she was working on a little book
about how to bring up children. She believed she
was an expert on the subject, and she meant to
become an expert on the problems of working
women.

This brought her next to the Jefferson Market
Courthouse, where she spent a Saturday night
observing the justice system in action. She had
brought her attorney, and they were present from
nine P.M. to three in the morning, Mrs. Belmont

wrapped in furs, under a hat so huge it had to be anchored by six jeweled hat pins. Spectators gasped at the sight.

When at last four pickets were brought into the courtroom, the prosecutor announced that they were not ready for trial — the workers would have to stay in jail till Monday night. Mrs. Belmont concluded this was meant as an object lesson to the others, a way of showing they could be jailed for three days whether guilty or not. Mrs. Belmont had no intention of allowing them to spend three days in jail, and bailed them out, putting up the Belmont mansion as security.

Several days later she told reporters, "During the six hours I spent in that police court I saw enough to convince me . . . beyond the smallest doubt of the absolute necessity for woman's suffrage . . . for the direct influence of women over judges, jury and policemen. . . . Every woman who sits complacently amid the comforts of her own home . . . and says, 'I have all the rights I want,' should spend one night at the Jefferson Market Court. She would then know that there are other women who have no rights which man or law or society recognizes."

Mrs. Belmont, Miss Morgan, Miss Dreier, and others sent out a call for "volunteer watchers," so that there would always be witnesses to mistreatment and arrest on the picket line. Watchers were strictly forbidden to picket, and were expected to belong to the "consumer" class. A special appeal was made to students at Barnard and Columbia.

At the same time a committee of lawyers was organized to represent strikers in court. This committee was headed by Miles Menander Dawson, who said, "We are most anxious to cooperate with the police and the courts. Our efforts are directed only toward seeing that the girls get an equal show along with the employers of peacefully winning the strike." Since Dawson was not a labor man, not a socialist firebrand, the League believed he stood a good chance of getting what they hoped for, fair play and a fair shake.

On the twenty-first of December Mrs. Belmont staged an "automobile parade," a tactic she had borrowed from English suffragists. Some fifteen long, luxurious vehicles honked their way through lower Manhattan with banners and posters declaring, THE WORKHOUSE IS NO ANSWER TO DEMANDS FOR JUSTICE, and THE POLICE ARE FOR OUR PROTECTION, NOT OUR ABUSE, and of course, VOTES FOR WOMEN.

Hungry, undernourished shirtwaist girls who had never before ridden in automobiles sat beside overfed society women, surrounded by rosewood panelling, leather upholstery, and fresh flowers held in slender glass vases fixed to the walls. These autos were driven by uniformed chauffeurs, except for Inez Milholland's, driven by herself. All along the line of march they were greeted by applause and cheers, while manufacturers watched from behind the windows of their offices with their hearts in their mouths. Was there no end to the trouble these misinformed ladies could cause?

Everyone had an opinion about the millionairesses. The labor press believed rich women were incapable of understanding the needs of working women. Those who spoke for management claimed they were an actual hindrance to the workers. "Society women who have hysterically taken up sides with the strikers are to blame for the prolongation of the strike," a magistrate said. "They have acted very unfairly. . . . Apparently they have ignored the manufacturers' side."

Were they there for sentimental reasons, as Emma Goldman claimed? Was it a form of hysteria, as the magistrate believed? Helen Marot, one of the League leaders, said it might well be true that upper-class women took part in the strike for sensational or personal motives — but once they came in contact with the strikers themselves their

motives changed. It was the courage of the workers and the hardships they endured that kept the
loyalty of the millionairesses.

As for Mary Dreier, she saw the strike as a
splendid demonstration of sisterhood. In her
opinion it had become a united front of women,
rich and poor together, demanding justice for all
women.

9

"WE WILL GO TO JAIL AGAIN AND WIN!"

A woman of seventy-nine — thin, wiry, dressed entirely in black, her snowy hair escaping from a flower-trimmed black bonnet — spoke to a strike rally in Philadelphia. "Get the spirit of revolt and be a woman," she told them. "It's not a Mrs. Belmont or an Anne Morgan that we want, but independent workers who will assert their rights."

She was a legendary labor agitator, Mary Harris Jones, known to working people throughout the country as Mother Jones. With no fixed home of her own she wandered from one industrial area to another. Where there was a strike she helped organize it, where there was no strike, she held "educational" meetings. The mines and mills of Pennsylvania were favorite haunts of hers because they employed so many women and little children, and she had earned an awesome reputation for mobilizing miners' wives, teaching them how to use hat pins and umbrellas. "God! It's the

old mother with her wild women!" the coal oper-
ators would cry whenever Mother Jones appeared.

Now she was helping to launch the shirtwaist
strike in Philadelphia. After weeks of waffling, on
December 20 it was finally under way — a blow
aimed directly at the manufacturers' association.
Who would make their shirtwaists now?

In New York, hunger and cold haunted the
picket lines. Arrests continued — seven hundred
so far — as did the fines, amounting in the end to
well over a million dollars. Rose Schneiderman
and Pauline Newman had toured the Northeast
in search of financial support from union locals,
but never got more than $600. It was seen as a
women's strike, and neither the ILGWU nor the
labor movement in general could ever bring
themselves to support it wholeheartedly.

Only a few thousand of the New York strikers
were still out. All of the others who had marched
together on that first thrilling day when the army
of workers took over the city, were back at their
old jobs in "settled" firms, or in other lines of
work, while some were too sick to work. But
Philadelphia had ten thousand striking shirtwaist
and dress workers. Even the lordly cutters were
with them.

Margaret Dreier Robins rushed there from

Chicago, bringing Agnes Nestor, national secretary of the International Glove Workers' Union, and one of the very few American women who have ever held a post as a national union officer. Mary Dreier joined them, and together they opened a League headquarters in the heart of the garment district.

Owners hired thugs to beat up the workers, while at the same time "lubricating the police . . . with gifts of waists and cigars," as the *Call* put it. Magistrates sentenced pickets to the county jail with or without provocation, and leaders of Philadelphia society persuaded a prominent clubman, Otto Mallery, to go bail for seven strikers.

College girls, especially those from nearby Bryn Mawr, marched on the picket lines, although an officer of Bryn Mawr claimed this was not possible — "Our girls do not do that sort of thing," she said. Sometimes a Bryn Mawr girl was mistaken for a striker, and hauled off to court, then to jail. When this happened to a graduate student named Martha Gruening, she did not take it silently.

She was charged with having caused a "near-riot" while on a picket line. Held on $500 bail, she spent a night in prison. Her father, a well-known New York physician, hurried to Philadelphia to bail her out, and as soon as she was free she in-

formed the newspapers that she was going to sue
the city for false arrest. She wasn't picketing, she
said, she was simply observing. Furthermore,
"My companions and I were locked in . . . a place
so filthy that we were afraid even to sit down."
The food was inedible, they were not allowed to
bathe, or make a phone call, and from start to finish, she continued, she was "treated as if I had actually been convicted of a crime."

Yet she was only awaiting trial. Was that justice? The Director of Public Safety denied everything, but when a committee of ministers
investigated the jail they corroborated Martha
Gruening's findings.

Other "college girls," and some of the older
women as well, marched on picket lines wearing
their academic gowns and caps. Some weeks later
they tried another novel strategy. Instead of
shouting at strikebreakers and risking arrest,
they handed out cards with the following message: "You are doing little more than starving to
death on the dollar-a-day wages that you are getting. Why not starve outside? Outside we have
fresh air and starvation is not so deadly. Inside, if
you don't starve to death, you will die of tuberculosis. Come on, get a little fresh air."

This mixture of wit and philosophy proved so
effective that several strikebreakers asked to be

taken to union headquarters, where they signed up and later joined the picket line. This was remarkable in itself — scab-workers turning their backs on their jobs to take part in a strike. It was even more remarkable that some were blacks, who had never been wanted in the garment trade, or for that matter in factory work of any kind, except as janitors. They occupied the lowest rung on the employment ladder, as live-in domestics or laundresses. Now, thanks to the shirtwaist strike, owners were grabbing every worker they could, and black women had a chance at factory jobs. That some refused to scab was a source of amazement to owners and unions alike.

There was still another unusual aspect to the Philadelphia strike. In New York young people were permitted by state law to start work at age sixteen, and although there were always a few underage children who had to be hidden in closets when the factory inspector came, on the whole the law was observed. In Pennsylvania, however, the legal age was fourteen, and the age limit was no barrier to the hiring of even younger children.

On December 22 the *Call* carried a front-page photo of four Philadelphia strikers — two twelve-year-old girls, and two others of thirteen and fourteen. And on Christmas Day a commit-

tee of strikers gave a party for seventy-five of the
tiniest pickets, all under fourteen. Their average
wage was forty-nine cents a day. Whether or not
the strike succeeded, it had already managed to
shine the light of publicity on Philadelphia's child
laborers.

Manufacturers in both cities were hurting
now; with Philadelphia factories shut down, the
big New York owners had no sure way of filling
their orders. Labor leaders pressed both sides,
union and owners, to work out some kind of compromise. After several sessions an agreement was
drawn up, with owners offering shorter hours; at
least four legal holidays a year with full pay; no
more petty fines and charges; wages in each shop
to be arranged between workers and owners,
meaning an end to the subcontracting system.

But the manufacturers' association still refused
to consider a union shop, since it was "nobody's
damn business what I pay my employees," as one
owner put it. However they were willing to listen
to any and all complaints on violations of the
agreement, would in fact welcome conferences
about any differences that could not be settled
between the individual shop and its workers. And
they would have no objection to hiring union
members. Wasn't that fair enough? Hadn't they
already made huge concessions?

Shop delegates met in New York on December 27 to hear the owners' proposal from the lips of a union official. He tried to impress on them the necessity of coming to some understanding with their bosses. And when questions were raised about union recognition, they were told, "Now, see here, don't get excited and excite others with you. We'll do the best we can under the circumstances."

That afternoon, during a snowstorm that stopped Manhattan traffic for days, the rank-and-file strikers were called to five mass meetings, where they would vote on the new proposal. According to the *Call*, these meetings were held so that no one could accuse union officials of selling out, of "driving the workers back to work like sheep to the slaughter."

So they came, in their wet torn shoes, hatless, coatless, half-starved, some almost dropping from weakness. They stood up on the tables, clung to the banisters, steadied themselves on windowsills, and hung onto balcony railings, as they listened to the speakers. Union officials told them what they had told shop delegates that morning — that the bosses were being generous, that compromise was necessary.

Then Morris Hillquit spoke, reminding them

that if the owners were to give in to every demand, yet manage to weaken or even destroy the
union, "they could and would restore the old condition of servitude in their shops, within a very
few weeks or months."

And then it was time to vote. But the workers
were too angry to vote. Once they understood the
owners' proposal, what it meant, and who was
trying to sell it to them — their leaders, the paid
officials of their own union — they smelled be-
trayal. What had they been fighting for all this
time, if not union recognition? There were cries
of, "Send it back, we will not consider it!" "We
refuse to vote on it!" "We will go to jail again and
win!"

The strike would continue. With Philadelphia
shut down, all they had to do was hold tight for
two more weeks — surely they could manage
two more weeks.

Word went out that the League was disap-
pointed with this unanimous decision, although
Mary Dreier denied it. The League wanted a real
settlement, she said, not a sham one, adding that
they had just begun to fight, which she had said
before. She was a religious woman; perhaps this
accounted for her belief that right would always
triumph over might. There were other League

members who felt distinctly let down by the strikers' decision. Union officials were furious, the mink brigade dismayed.

It was as if all their efforts on behalf of the shirtwaist workers — the money spent, the time, the sympathy poured out — had gone for nothing. How important was union recognition? Wasn't half a loaf better than none?

The *Times* had a similar change of heart. On their editorial page they now claimed the remaining strikers were not sincere in saying they wanted the closed shop in order to assure better working conditions. "They want the closed shop to prevent others taking the wages they scorn," said the *Times*. "When they strike for the closed shop they are not striking for any right of their own, but to take away the right of working from all but their own members."

From then on, articles in the *Times* tended to show the strikers in an unfavorable light, reporting that rotten eggs were thrown at owners and strikebreakers. That an eighteen-year-old paid her $10 fine entirely in pennies, "causing great annoyance in the court." That strikers often resorted to violence, in one case requiring a half-dozen policemen to restore order: "Around noontime yesterday the telephone bell in the Mercer Street Station rang and a voice asked

for reserves to be sent to Third and Mercer
Streets . . . as a riot was going on there."

It was left to the *Call* to report the strikers'
side — factory-owners sending police and scabs
to invade union meetings, at night, and without a
warrant; a cutter, coming downstairs from a meeting of his union, attacked in the street and beaten
into insensibility.

In Clinton Hall it was clear that the strikers
could not go on much longer without facing actual starvation. The League appealed to neighborhood grocers, hoping for supplies that would
provide some kind of breakfast. A theater owner
promised half the profits of his new play to the
shirtwaist girls. The Women's Committee of the
Socialist Party gave them a dance in a brightly lit
hall, with good music, and a good floor, and on
another day held a reception to honor girls coming back from imprisonment at Blackwell's Island. And the *Call* offered to put out a special
edition for them, all profits to go to the strike
fund.

Each of these efforts to raise the spirits of the
remaining strikers helped for a time, yet all were
marred by rumors that vibrated throughout the
garment district — that the strike was about to
be called off, which union men continued to deny,
every denial making it seem more likely.

On December 29 the special issue of the *Call* was ready for distribution. It had been put together by several League members with the help of strikers, and carried the history of the strike along with appeals for contributions, photos of leading figures, bits of poetry, as well as a cartoon showing a very small striker and a large thug standing before a magistrate. The thug, grinning broadly, says, "Please protect me, Mr. Judge! She threatened to beat me up!"

There was also a wistful letter. Under the title, "My Daughter Is Not a Scab!" the writer explained that Anna Zeitz was sick, "unable to proceed with the work of the struggle she and you have started. . . . The only thing I want to point out is that SHE IS NOT A SCAB and I hope you will not suspect anything of this kind. . . . In conclusion, be true! Stand shoulder to shoulder until you win! I am with you." It was signed by S. Zeitz, the father of Anna, a Triangle striker.

Now hundreds of workers and college girls took to the streets as "newsies," with the temperature at five degrees above zero on the coldest day of an exceptionally cold winter. The newsies had broad white sashes across their shoulders, and bundles of papers under their arms that were supposed to sell for five cents apiece. Buyers would be encouraged to pay more, preferably much more, since every penny was destined for the strike fund.

Some headed straight for Wall Street, even to the offices of J. P. Morgan & Co., where one copy was sold for a dollar. Others traveled uptown to Columbia University, or to the Waldorf-Astoria, or Hoffman House, where the manufacturers' association had its headquarters. In the better parts of town there was little sympathy for the strike. People said if the girls were in need they had only to go back to their machines. One of the newsies remembered starting out near Twenty-third Street, then making her way downtown to a poorer section, "and the further I went the easier it became to dispose of my load. Here the restaurant keepers allowed me to enter, warm up a bit and sell my papers, while in the swell places I was not permitted to enter the vestibule."

At the Third Street Vaudeville House two strikers sold $76 worth of papers in three evenings, and on Broadway a "rich gentleman" gave a five-dollar gold piece for a single issue. Altogether some 50,000 copies were sold, bringing more than five thousand much-needed dollars to the strike fund.

Hopes were high in Philadelphia, where the strike was new and fresh. Inez Milholland had gone there and managed to get herself arrested, along with a young Army lieutenant, Henry Turney. The pair were charged with causing a crowd to assemble. As the arresting officer explained, this crowd of a hundred and fifty girls handled him so roughly that all the buttons were torn from the coat of his uniform. The evening newspaper that carried the story noted Miss Milholland's "furs and modish costume," and printed a charming picture of her.

But in New York the strike was an old story. And in Clinton Hall the lines of applicants for strike benefits extended from the ground floor to the fourth, with people standing four abreast.

10

THE NEW YEAR

The employers' association announced that there would be no more conferences, no more arbitration. They were finished with conferences and arbitration. So far as they were concerned the strike would be over only when the union admitted defeat.

Members of the employers' association dominated the industry and set its tone. But they could not keep the owners of small shops, the little "insects" of businesses, from sneaking into Clinton Hall to sign agreements and invite their old workers back, and they continued to do so. What were these agreements worth? People wondered about it, but all the same there were workers who did go back, even now. Hunger drove them back.

Others proudly refused to go. Like Clara Lemlich, who had given all her savings to the strike fund, they were mostly older, more experienced workers, and they saw the strike in visionary terms. It was a movement without leaders, without a selfish few seeking ends of their own; they were all leaders, the strikers believed, and they were part of a historical process whose goal was freedom for the generations still to come. One of them told a journalist, "my heart weeps for the younger girls . . . that they should find life so hard and miserable when they are so young; that they should begin to lose their red cheeks from the very moment they land in America." By holding out, not for better wages and hours, but for union recognition, they were building a future for others.

Fanny Zinsher was another of the true believers, twenty years old and as quiet and serious as Clara was impulsive. A reporter for the *Survey* interviewed Fanny and told her story — how she'd been working at the Triangle, and joined the strike eighteen weeks ago. How she spoke to one of the prostitutes, and was arrested by an officer who "pinched her arm black and blue as he dragged this dangerous criminal to court." Fanny Zinsher had been working for the strike ever since, working harder than she ever did over a sewing machine, either giving fund-raising talks to clubs and trade unions, or on duty at Clinton Hall from early morning till eleven at night. She, too, gave all the money she had, the savings that were supposed to pay for an American education, to the strike fund. Now her greatest fear was that she would be forced back into one of the settled shops while the union still needed her, for the workers' "only hope of decent human living is in sticking together."

The union men found such sentiments laughable. Benjamin Stolberg of the ILGWU dismissed the Fanny Zinshers and Clara Lemlichs as "Chickens in a China Shop." With their "chronic exaltation over the Class-Conscious Worker and the Toiling Masses," these female activists made "life miserable for nearly every leader in the union," he continues. They, the male officials, were cool and level-headed bureaucrats in his opinion, and they carried out their strike duties to the best of their abilities, while reacting to the antics of the women with bored indifference and the occasional heavy-handed joke.

Apparently it did not occur to Stolberg that the chronic exaltation of the strikers was the source of their strength. It kept them warm on the picket lines, it fueled their resistance to thugs and police, and hardened them during confinement in the Tombs. Thanks to chronic exaltation they had already forced hundreds of small employers to settle on their terms, and compelled the union to turn down the seductive offers of the owners' association. The strike continued now only because the workers had voted it to continue, knowing they might not win everything they wanted, might not win anything at all. It was the principle that mattered, the principle of union recognition, and their willingness to sacrifice, to go hungry for it, was due to chronic exaltation, which meant nerve, faith, a romantic belief that they were part of an important cause.

In the Old World, the voices of Jewish women were never heard beyond the household or the family-owned business, but in America the daughters learned in the course of the shirtwaist strike how to influence events outside the home. When it was over and they had returned to their machines, they would do so with a new sense of their own worth. Never again would the bosses find it quite so easy to bully them. And they in turn would be less likely to defer to the judgments of men, having learned that the men were not gods, not infallible, perhaps no wiser or better than women.

During this same period, the start of the new year, plans were being made for one last rally, one final meeting of the strike community, to be held at Carnegie Hall. Most of the arranging was done by a committee of twelve socialist women, their stated purpose being to honor those who had been jailed or sent to the workhouse, and to protest the system that allowed such injustice.

The mink brigade participated but was wary of this rally. It was in fact wary of the socialist women, who had already proclaimed their refusal to cooperate with their "bourgeois sisters," the suffragists. Each group believed the other was using the strike for its own purposes — the socialists pushing a political agenda, the suffragists concerned only with getting votes for women, after which they would lose all interest in factory workers.

While these tensions simmered just beneath the surface, the surface itself was calm — to the press and the owners' association, the strikers and their supporters showed a united front. But as the date of the rally approached, people on both sides became somewhat more outspoken. There were small disturbances in the calm surface, cracks here and there in the united front.

A worker described a meeting at Clinton Hall when the question of speakers came up: "'We don't want any agitators,' protested one of the [ladies]. 'We are here to see that the Carnegie meeting has the tone of respectability attached to it.' It goes without saying she means the Socialists. I couldn't help wondering why the rich are so afraid of them."

A contingent of workers went to Alva Belmont's home to ask about her real purpose in supporting the strike. When she refused to see them they wrote out two questions that her secretary was to bring to her: "Are you interested in strikers because they are possible suffragists or because they are workers in trouble?" And, "Do you believe the interests of the employers and workers are identical or could ever be identical?" The secretary brought back word that Mrs. Belmont was too busy to answer. The strikers requested a future meeting but were told it would not be possible.

All the same the press knew nothing about it. When the audience filled Carnegie Hall on the second of January, Anne Morgan was there, and Carrie Chapman Catt, representing the National Woman Suffrage League, and the crusading rabbi Stephen Wise, and George Kirchwey, Dean of the Columbia Law School, along with Mrs. Belmont and other members of the mink brigade.

Some 350 workers sat on the brightly lit stage wearing wide strips of paper with the word ARRESTED in huge black letters. In their front row were twenty who had been sent to the workhouse, all wearing streamers over their shoulders that read, *I Am a Criminal*.

Signs distributed throughout the hall bore

such messages as: THE WORKHOUSE IS NO AN-
SWER TO A DEMAND FOR JUSTICE, and PEACEFUL
PICKETING IS THE RIGHT OF EVERY WORKER.
There were no suffrage messages. Suffrage had
had its rallies. The themes that night were police
brutality and corruption in the courts — the sick-
nesses of the social order.

There were speeches, one by Miles Dawson
who with other lawyers had been fighting the
battles of the strikers before the magistrates, "because the weakest and most defenseless of our
people have been denied the equal protection of
the law."

Leonora O'Reilly spoke, passionate as always,
declaring that this strike had done more to make
people aware of common bonds of kinship than
the preaching of all the churches had done in
years. When she introduced Rosie Perr the audience gasped because she was so little, so childlike
in appearance, her hair worn in a long braid
down her back. She told about being taken to the
station house as a witness when she asked a police captain to arrest a thug who had slapped her
friend. Instead of acting as a witness, she was ac-
cused of having assaulted a scab, and sentenced
to five days in the workhouse before she ever
opened her mouth.

Then Morris Hillquit spoke, praising the strik-

ers for forming a powerful union almost overnight and fighting gallantly to maintain it. Stopping once in mid-speech, he pointed to those on
the stage — "women whose imprisonment was an
honor" — and applause like thunderclaps continued for several minutes. Hillquit then brought up
the greed of the owners, and the "servitude" of
the workers. He stressed the importance of the
union shop, but went on to explain that the union
alone was powerless to correct social injustice.

It was a long speech, repeating themes that
had been heard before. Nevertheless, it had an
unforeseen effect on the women of the mink
brigade. Anne Morgan, in particular, found it in-
flammatory. The next day she stormed out of the
League, and released a tirade to the press accusing Hillquit, O'Reilly, and others of indoctrinat-
ing the girls with "the fanatical doctrines of
Socialism."

On its editorial page the *Call* replied, "The real
danger to the working girls lies in the pretended
friendship of the Miss Morgans, who come down
from the height of their pedestals to preach iden-
tity of interests to the little daughters of the people." Morris Hillquit, apparently baffled, said he
had not spoken as a socialist, but had no desire to
conceal his socialist views.

It is hard to account for Anne Morgan's sud-

den realization that people like O'Reilly and
Hillquit were socialists. Just as Hillquit said, he
had never concealed it, and the same was true for
the rest of the union men, socialists all, who had
likewise never concealed it. The entire East Side,
for that matter, was already indoctrinated with
socialism, and if Anne Morgan was unaware of
this fact, it could only be because she failed to understand either the ILGWU, or the world of the
Lower East Side.

What she did understand was that people like
herself were being attacked on all sides for trying
to help with the strike. Now tensions that had
simmered under the surface of the united front
were out in the open. Many of the millionairesses
withdrew their support. Suffragists and settlement workers grew increasingly cool. Socialist
women, who had worked hard from the start, col-
lecting strike funds when most other sources
dried up, expressed resentments they had more
or less kept to themselves until now. They
claimed they were never appreciated, that the
well-to-do women got all the credit, all the newspaper coverage. "There has never been a more
humiliating position in the history of the labor
movement than that occupied by the Socialist
women in the shirtwaist strike," according to a
letter in the *Call*.

None of this infighting seemed to trouble Mrs. Belmont. As for Anne Morgan, who had abandoned the League because of its ties to the fanatical union, she, too, remained a friend of the strikers, although she did so for the wrong reasons. She pitied them, saw them as touchingly innocent, but mindless. "It is very reprehensible," she said, "for Socialists to take advantage of these poor girls in these times, and when the working people are in such dire straits. . . . "

To her credit, Mrs. Belmont knew better. When asked if she didn't find the majority of the strikers helpless and ignorant, she replied, "They are not ignorant. They are very well educated indeed, and many of them have read and thought a great deal. And they will not be helpless any longer once they are allowed to vote, and that brings us, as everything does, back to the suffrage question."

Her reasons for helping the strikers were more than merely sentimental, more even than a desire for excitement. Although her life had been a succession of triumphs, it was also a succession of snubs, first by Mobile, Alabama, then by New York society. Even before that, in a world managed by men she had the misfortune of being born to second-class citizenship. She would have to fight her way out. Women from all walks of life

would have to join her, for they, too, were second-
class citizens. She never saw suffrage and the
rights of women workers as competing causes,
but as two battlefronts in a single war.

Soon after the Carnegie Hall rally, a meeting
took place that showed Alva Belmont at her most
militant. A group of women schoolteachers were
eager to help the shirtwaist girls, and she told
them precisely how to do it: "Let all the working
women of the city come together," she said. "Let
them agree upon a date. Let them go upon a sympathetic strike on that date, and let them remain
on strike until the striking shirtwaist makers win
their fight completely."

Although it may well have been true that a
citywide strike of all female workers would effec-
tively end the shirtwaist strike, it was an idea far
ahead of its time, and not at all what the schoolteachers had in mind. They said they were in
favor of no such thing.

Mrs. Belmont bought stock in a cooperative
factory for the making of shirtwaists under strict
union supervision. She sold tickets for a theater
performance to benefit the strikers, and she continued, as before, to make headlines whatever she
did. But the days of the strike were numbered
now. Local grocers who had been supplying food
on credit were facing bankruptcy, and forced to

withdraw their help. By mid-January, strikers
were doing daily picket duty on little or no food,
in a city blanketed by snow twelve inches deep
and whipped by winds of forty miles an hour.

The union sent them out in teams of two, door-
to-door throughout the tenements of the Lower
East Side to ask for money. At League headquarters a committee of prominent Italians voted to
appeal for aid in Italian-language newspapers;
they, too, would arrange for house-to-house can-
vassing in the Italian district — desperate measures, equaled only by the desperation of the
factory owners. With the busy season ready to
peak in April, and Philadelphia still on strike,
their ears rang with "the clamor of customers for
guarantees that their orders will be filled," as the
Call put it.

One of the largest firms, the Bijou, was so determined to get its orders out that they hired 150
policemen to keep strikers away from their workers; policemen and workers were to sleep and eat
in the factory till the strike came to an end.
Meanwhile firms that had settled early on with
the union were conveniently "forgetting" their
agreements.

Others, like Triangle, which had no intention
of recognizing the union, claimed their motives
were purely idealistic: "We are perfectly willing

that those of our workers who so desire shall belong to the union," they said, "but we will not deal
with the union leaders nor discriminate against
the workers who do not join the union. . . . We
sympathize with the liberty-loving employee."
Triangle reopened its New York factory, and put
a notice in the paper promising shirtwaist makers
fifteen to twenty dollars a week along with free
lunch and dancing during the noon hour. There
were firms that promised to take workers door-
to-door by private automobile.

Members of the manufacturers' association
were now putting together a blacklist, the *Call*
said, in order to prevent the last of the strikers
from regaining their jobs "after they are beaten."

11

TRIANGLE SETTLES

Although the AFL claimed that they welcomed into their ranks "all labor without regard to creed, color, sex, race or nationality," their union locals found ingenious ways to exclude black workers. Some demanded high initiation fees that black men were unable to pay, others simply closed their apprenticeship programs to blacks, and without proper training they were unable to qualify for membership.

So black women were doubly handicapped. Like the men, they were kept out of unions that were theoretically open to all workers, and like white women they were pushed aside because of their sex. Yet unless they could gain a foothold in the unions, black women were likely to remain forever in the most menial jobs, working as either live-in domestics, or as scrubbers and sweepers of factory floors.

In January of 1910, an editorial in a black

weekly, the *New York Age*, boasted of having re-
cruited "colored girls" as ironers with shirtwaist
firms that were still on strike. They had been
asked not to accept advertisements for strikebreakers, the *Age* continued, but had done so all
the same. Black women were never wanted by
the garment trade, and now that they had a
chance to break in, "Why should negro working
girls pull white working girls' chestnuts out of the
fire?"

The day after this editorial was published,
members of the Cosmopolitan Club — white as
well as black, reformers and liberals who usually
met in the homes of black society leaders — held
an emergency meeting at a Brooklyn church.
They passed a resolution urging the black woman
worker "to refrain from injuring other working
women, and whenever possible, to ally herself
with the cause of union labor."

A Brooklyn reader responded to that same editorial in the *Age*. His letter pointed out what
everyone already knew, that "colored shirtwaist
makers could not get into the union and were
likewise not permitted by the union to work in
the shops."

Margaret Dreier Robins was one of many progressives who had been debating the issue of race
prejudice for years. She could not deny its exis-

tence, yet when she saw the Brooklyn reader's letter it shamed her enough so that she, too, wrote a letter, one that tried to put the best face on an ugly situation: "Permit me to say that both in New York and . . . Philadelphia, two of the most devoted pickets are colored girls, for they have not only been able to persuade the girls of their own race and color to stand by their sisters, but they have also been most successful in persuading the white girls to stand by them. In the early days of the strike in New York, a colored girl went to the headquarters of the . . . League not quite certain of her welcome, but she had only appeared in the doorway when a young Russian Jewess ran up to her, and holding out both hands said with greatest enthusiasm, 'I am so glad you have joined us, I am so glad you have joined us.'"

Another League woman, Elizabeth Dutcher, wrote to the magazine *Horizon:* "In New York, colored girls are not only members of the union, but they have been prominent in the union. One colored girl has been secretary of her shop organization all through the strike and has been very frequently at the union headquarters doing responsible work."

Horizon, which was founded and edited by the black scholar W. E. B. Du Bois, thanked Miss Dutcher for writing and urged all black Americans to study her words, especially those who "are assisting in the present insidious effort to make our people Ishmaelites in the world of labor, or as someone has put it, to make us 'Cossacks' of America."

While these letters were being exchanged, it was still possible that the shirtwaist strikers might win their demand for union recognition — and if they did, the future of black workers in the industry would depend on the ILGWU's willingness to recruit them. Mrs. Robins knew this, just as she must have known that two or three black union members did not absolve the union of racism.

In May of that year the national League's executive board held a post-strike meeting at which the gains and losses of the uprising were examined. And when they came to the matter of black workers, their consciences pricked them sufficiently that they pledged to do something about organizing black women. Ten years were to pass before anything much was done, however. The League's dependence on the AFL had made such efforts practically impossible.

January was a depressing month; there was nothing good to report. Newspapers claimed only five hundred strikers were left, although the number was probably closer to three thousand.

Pickets were still bullied and arrested. A worker in one of the settled shops remembered dancing to phonograph music during the lunch break, while from the streets below she heard the screams of strikers being manhandled by thugs.

In early February, Philadelphia's strike was settled by arbitration. Even Triangle had settled by then — a partial settlement, one that never recognized the union. Another demand they refused to consider was for open and unlocked doors leading from their three upper floors to the street; foremen were accustomed to locking these doors, keeping workers in and union organizers out. And Triangle made no promises about the blacklisting of strike leaders. Having settled on their own terms, they gave all their energies to making shirtwaists and money.

More than a year was to pass before the day in March 1911 when onlookers noticed wisps of smoke coming out of the Asch Building, where Triangle occupied three top floors. Fire engines shrieked. Soon the whole eighth floor spouted jets of flame. Then something resembling a bale of dress goods was thrown from a tenth floor window. When a breeze tossed open the cloth, the crowd saw inside it the body of a girl.

It took only minutes for the entire building to be engulfed. There was no sprinkler system, doors opened inward if they opened at all, and one door did not, while the single fire escape ended five feet above the ground, with an iron spike fence below it. One after another, fear-crazed women came to the windows, said their prayers, and jumped to their deaths. "They didn't want to jump," one of the survivors said later. "They were afraid. They were . . . putting rags over their eyes so they could not see. They said it was better to be smashed than burned. . . . They wanted to be identified." Fifty-eight women who could not bring themselves to jump had crawled into a room on the ninth floor, where their burnt bodies were later found with the faces raised toward the one small window. A total of 146 workers died, either burnt to black ashes, or smashed by the pavement.

A reporter who covered the fire wrote that he looked upon the dead and remembered these girls were the shirtwaist makers. "I remembered their great strike of last year in which the same girls had demanded more sanitary conditions and more safety precautions in the shops. Their dead bodies were the answer."

For years, decades to come, people would re-member the tragedy that was the Triangle fire, even people who were too young to remember — the memories their parents had would be impressed so deeply on their minds that it seemed they, too, had lived through that terrible time.

Rose Schneiderman wept unashamedly when she addressed a memorial service, held at the Metropolitan Opera House under the sponsorship of the League: "This is not the first time girls have been burned alive in this city. . . . Every year thousands of us are maimed. The life of men and women is so cheap and property is so sacred!"

The service was followed by a funeral parade, members of the New York League marching with workers, in utter silence, under a drenching rain, behind a hearse that symbolized all the young lives that had ended in flames.

But these events took place a little over one year later. In February of 1910, they were unforeseen, unimagined. People were aware only that the long fight was stumbling to a close, that like it or not the time had come for both sides to approach one another. With this in mind Mrs. Belmont invited Anne Morgan, Mary Dreier, Clara Lemlich, John Dyche, and all the manufacturers who had taken their workers back, to a "Peace Luncheon" at Delmonico, the most elegant restaurant in Manhattan.

Clara Lemlich had been working and speaking

nonstop since the start of the strike, and she was exhausted now, drained of emotional energy, perhaps on the brink of nervous breakdown. But this was an occasion not to be missed. Coming in through the restaurant's Fifth Avenue entrance, Mrs. Belmont's guests crossed the thick carpeting of the main dining room, furnished in Louis XVI style, its walls covered by panels of green and yellow satin. Then they climbed the staircase to a private room — quantities of flowers, heavily starched linen on the tables, a color scheme of pinks and reds.

Although many manufacturers had agreed to come, only a half-dozen actually showed up. There was an air of informality. The speeches were short, almost conversational in tone. Clara did not speak, however. When she looked back on that part of her life she was amazed at how many speeches she'd already made, how much newsprint had been used to describe them: "I read about them now — all those important people and Clara Lemlich here, Clara Lemlich there!" Her hands would fly to her head whenever she thought about it later. On this day she was one of those who listened.

People were talking about the use of union labels on garments made by unionized shops.

"Won't you all promise to wear only union shirt-waists for one year?" asked Mrs. Belmont, raising her hand as an example.

"All those that I can get in this country," Anne Morgan replied, somewhat tactlessly. Clara Lemlich could not afford to buy shirtwaists in Paris or London, any more than she could visit Paris or London. The most she could hope for was a chance to get out of New York and recover her health.

The Rev. Mr. Percy Grant told the guests about a visit two years earlier by a British suffragist, who found American women disappointing because they had no interest in public questions. Since then, he said, "a great change has occurred, the happiest of changes, for our women are showing that they do take an interest in the life, labors, and demands of thousands of working women and girls." Then refreshments were served, and everyone broke bread together, and two weeks later the strike was officially over.

This happened quietly, with none of the passion that marked its beginning. Thugs and police went back to their normal occupations; the college girls, loyal to the last, went back to theirs, as did the socialites and members of the press, and for the time being the Lower East Side was left to those whose home it was.

Clara Lemlich went to the country for a long rest. When she returned she found herself black-listed, one of several strike leaders who for years to come could find work in the industry only under fictitious names.

The direct results of the strike were modest: shorter hours, a small increase in pay, overtime wages, and an end to the humiliation of petty fines, rental payments for machines, chairs, lockers, etc. Over three hundred firms had settled, but nineteen did so on a compromise basis, refusing a union shop, and some declined to recognize that any union existed.

Yet there were more than 20,000 members added to the ranks of the ILGWU, now well on its way to becoming a mass organization. It was also the nation's first permanent union of working women, one that had brought a powerful industry to a halt for thirteen weeks. Even Samuel Gompers was compelled to recognize "the extent to which women are taking up with industrial life . . . and the capacity of women as strikers to suffer, to do, and to dare in support of their rights."

Thanks to publicity generated by the League, the college girls, and the mink brigade, corruption in both the police department and the city's judicial system was brought to the nation's attention by a sympathetic press. In the same way, the problems of workers, and of working women in particular, erupted into public consciousness — an entire class of people, once invisible, made suddenly real and immediate.

The strike had an enormous impact on the labor movement as a whole, and especially the garment trades. In 1910, some 60,000 workers in New York's menswear industry marched on picket lines, eventually winning something very like a closed shop agreement. A general strike of men's clothing workers in Chicago followed, and others in Cleveland and Milwaukee. These uprisings laid the foundation for stable and lasting unions in the garment trades, and all of this had been ignited by the shirtwaist strike.

There were important changes within the community of East Side Jews, a people who hungered for acceptance, who cherished the hope that in the New World they could become as American as any other recent immigrants. They had had mud flung at them in the form of accusations that they were breeders of crime. Then their daughters erupted into unionism. They made demands, paraded through the streets, flung eggs at other workers, for which they were beaten and jailed and sent to the workhouse. Yet somehow they had emerged as national heroines.

Afterward, people talked about "our wonderful fervent girls," whose sudden, emotional outburst brought a new sense of what immigrants could accomplish. The Italians were part of this; Italian girls and Jewish girls, who had marched side by side on picket lines, formed lasting friendships there. They, too, were New York's daughters.

EPILOGUE

Rose Schneiderman came to national prominence as a labor organizer and social reformer. A long and close friendship with Eleanor Roosevelt began when Mrs. Roosevelt joined the League in 1922, and associates of Franklin Roosevelt believed the president's liberal views on labor relations were shaped in large part by Rose Schneiderman. When she died, the *New York Times* described her as a tiny bundle of social dynamite, who "did more to upgrade the dignity and living standards of working women than any other American."

For the rest of her long life Clara Lemlich was a union stalwart, although never again in a position of leadership. She did go to France after all. As one of the earliest anti-fascist activists, she attended a 1934 International Women's Congress Against War and Fascism in Paris, then went on to Russia, "the country where they wouldn't even let me go to school."

Having entered the shirtwaist strike with little preparation or experience, the Women's Trade Union League emerged as a force to be reckoned with, especially in the garment trades. Nevertheless, and despite the public pronouncements of Samuel Gompers, the AFL never fully accepted either the League, or the women it represented. Margaret Dreier Robins, a personal friend of the Gompers family, had to admit that the "arrogance and contempt" of AFL leaders for working women made her blood boil.

Mrs. Robins was the glue that held the League together during the years of her presidency; she supported it financially out of her personal fortune — "I never earned a dollar of it and I recognize that I hold it in trust," she once said — and she smoothed over ongoing differences between workers and "ladies." In 1914, at her suggestion, a training program was set up in Chicago to prepare women for leadership roles in trade unions. In succeeding years the League was instrumental in securing labor legislation that protected women and children — the eight-hour day, for example, the abolition of child labor, factory inspection laws, and a minimum wage.

When J. P. Morgan died on the eve of World War I, he left his daughter Anne a somewhat modest fortune that she used to buy a villa near

Paris. From then on she devoted her restless energies to relief and reconstruction in postwar France. To raise funds, she sponsored a prizefight in Madison Square Garden, and was photographed in the ring between the contestants, Bennie Leonard and Ritchie Mitchell. There was considerable criticism — *Clergy Flay Anne Morgan*, according to one newspaper — but the match netted close to $70,000.

Thanks to a lifetime annuity from Mary Dreier, Leonora O'Reilly was able to work full-time for the League. She was a founding member of the NAACP, continually active in the Socialist party, and a committed suffragist. Her health was poor, however, and after World War I she retired from public life, perhaps having burned herself out.

Inez Milholland went to law school, then joined a Manhattan firm, although her chief interests were still suffrage and reform causes. Living in Greenwich Village among radicals, artists, and bohemians, she fell in and out of love and was in no hurry to marry. Yet she did marry. He was an adventurous Dutch businessman, Eugen Boissevain, who took pride in his role as the husband of a gallant feminist leader. Three years later she was diagnosed as having pernicious anemia, but insisted on continuing with a speaking tour in support of women's suffrage. In Los Angeles she collapsed on the platform and died before her thirtieth birthday. Eugen Boissevain later married the poet Edna St. Vincent Millay.

After the Triangle fire, Mary Dreier was one of nine experts assigned to study New York State factories. Investigating fire prevention, safety standards, and industrial disease, they drafted legislation that revolutionized the state's labor laws. Then Miss Dreier turned her attention to the suffrage campaign. As she explained to Leonora O'Reilly, "The attitude of the labor men to the working women has changed me from being an ardent supporter of labor to a somewhat rabid supporter of women and to feel that the enfranchisement of women and especially my working-class sisters is the supreme issue."

Mary Dreier served on many government boards and private organizations concerned with labor and women — gentle, utterly sincere, she remained politically active until her death at eighty-eight.

The flamboyant Mrs. Belmont devoted the rest of her life and much of her fortune to feminist causes. She opened Marble House, her Newport mansion, for a suffrage conference, to the dismay of her head butler who believed these were the sort of people who would steal anything. In 1912, when she was almost sixty, she led a division of the great Women's Vote parade down the length of Fifth Avenue, a three-mile march. There were brass bands and mounted police and thousands of women from all over the country, with Mrs. Belmont walking every step of the way. A reporter noted that the woman beside her was "Rebecca Goldstein, who runs a sewing machine in a shirtwaist shop."

Surely this was the most significant gain of the uprising, its revelation of the power that lies in sisterhood, for no band of millionaire men has ever gone to the aid of male workers, yet women of all classes clasped hands and joined forces during the shirtwaist strike.

In the black winter of 1909
When we froze and bled on the picket line
We showed the world that women could fight,
And we rose and we won with women's might.

Hail! the waistmakers of nineteen nine,
Making their stand on the picket line,
Breaking the power of those who reign,
Pointing the way, smashing the chain.

BIBLIOGRAPHY

Adams, Graham. *Age of Industrial Violence.* New York: Columbia University Press, 1966.

Allen, Frederick Lewis. *The Big Change: America Transforms Itself 1900–1950.* New York: Harper & Brothers, 1952.

Balsan, Consuelo Vanderbilt. *The Glitter and the Gold.* New York: Harper & Brothers, 1952.

Baxandall, Rosalyn. *America's Working Women.* New York: Random House, 1976.

Dye, Nancy Schrom. *As Sisters and As Equals: Feminism, Unionism and the Women's Trade Union League of New York.* Columbia, MO: University of Missouri Press, 1980.

Flexner, Eleanor. *A Century of Struggle: The Woman's Rights Movement in the United States.* New York: Atheneum, 1971.

Foner, Philip. *Women and the American Labor Movement: From the First Trade Unions to the Present.* New York: Free Press, 1979.

Glenn, Susan. *Daughters of the Shtetl.* Ithaca: Cornell University Press, 1990.

Howe, Irving. *World of Our Fathers.* New York: Harcourt Brace Jovanovich, 1976.

Jensen, Joan M., and Sue Davidson, eds. *A Needle, a Bobbin, a Strike: Women Needleworkers in America.* Philadelphia: Temple University Press, 1984.

Kessner, Thomas. *The Golden Door.* New York: Oxford University Press, 1977.

Laslett, John. *Labor and the Left.* New York: Basic Books, 1970.

Levine, Louis. *The Women's Garment Workers.* New York: B.W. Huebsch, 1924.

Malkiel, Theresa Serber. *The Diary of a Shirtwaist Striker.* Cooperative Press, 1910. Reprinted by ILR Press, School of Industrial and Labor Relations, Cornell University, 1990.

Mandel, Bernard. *Samuel Gompers.* Yellow Springs, OH: Antioch Press, 1963.

Payne, Elizabeth Anne. *Reform, Labor, and Feminism: Margaret Dreier Robins and the National Women's Trade Union League.* Urbana: University of Illinois Press, 1988.

Raban, Jonathan. *Hunting Mister Heartbreak: A Discovery of America.* New York: HarperCollins, 1991.

Rischin, Moses. *The Promised City: New York's Jews, 1870–1914.* Cambridge: Harvard University Press, 1962.

Stein, Leon. *The Triangle Fire.* Philadelphia: J.B. Lippincott, 1962.

Tax, Meredith. *The Rising of the Women.* New York: Monthly Review Press, 1980.

Van Vorst, Marie, and Bessie Van Vorst. *The Woman Who Toils.* New York: Doubleday, Page & Co., 1903.

Wertheimer, Barbara M. *We Were There: The Story of Working Women in America.* New York: Pantheon Books, 1977.

For contemporary newspaper accounts of the strike see: *The New York Times; The New York Call; Philadelphia Evening Bulletin.*

For contemporary periodicals: *The Survey; McClure's Magazine; Collier's; The Outlook; Literary Digest; The World Today; Independent.*

INDEX

Photo Credits